To Aunty Helen,

Merry Christmas 1983

Love
from

Eм.

Alistair

KU-207-717

Western Australia

LOOKING WEST

Richard Woldendorp

Publisher's Note

It is not easy to write or photograph Western Australia and say, 'That's it'. There is always more that could have been said. But I hope that his book will give an impression of the character and feelings of this enormous State.

I thank all the people that have assisted in getting the material for this book—in particular the Government of Western Australia for their co-operation and interest; M.M.A. who arranged so many journeys through the interior; and the sponsors who have shown their confidence and goodwill and made the project possible:—

M. G. Kailis Exports Pty. Ltd.,
MacRobertson Miller Airline Services
Mt. Newman Mining Co. Pty. Ltd.
Transfield (W.A.) Pty. Ltd.
Walkabout Hotels
Westralian Farmers Co-operative.

The book has been produced in association with West Coast Holdings Limited.

Published in Western Australia
by Day Dawn Press;
P.O. Box M939, Perth, W.A.

First Published 1977.

Copyright © R. L. Woldendorp

This book is copyright.
Apart from any fair dealing
for the purposes of private study,
research, criticism or review,
as permitted under the Copyright Act,
no part may be reproduced
by any process without written permission.
Enquiries should be made to the publisher.

National Library of Australia
Cataloguing-in-publication data
Woldendorp, Richard Leo, 1927
Day Dawn Press
ISBN 0 9596934 0 8

Designer: Peter Joughin

Printed in Singapore by
Toppan Printing Co. Pte. Ltd.
Typeset in Western Australia by
Waters Typographic House, North Fremantle

Western Australia

LOOKING WEST

History
150 years of rapid growth
Geoffrey Bolton
Professor of History
at the Murdoch University.
He has written several books
on history beginning with
'The Life of Alexander Forrest.'

Social
People at work and play
Kirwan Ward
Well known journalist,
world traveller, radio commentator,
script writer and author
of seven books.

Economy
Mining, industry and
the man on the land
Don Lipscombe
Writer on Western Australia
for the London Financial Times
and publishes the mining letter—
'Western Intelligence Report.'

Nature
The land, flora & fauna
Philip Bodeker
Journalist with the Daily News.
Author of the Sangroper Guide
and the Sandgropers Trail.

Foreword

It is an old truism that the visitor to any locality usually goes further and sees more than the local resident. Richard Woldendorp is no visitor to Western Australia. He has been here long enough to qualify as a dinkum Sandgroper . . . but he does have a background in another country, and it enables him to use the lens of his camera with rather more object-ivity and artistry and enthusiasm—and, strangely enough, more love—than most native-born Western Australians.

I worked with Richard for several years in all parts of the State and in just about every conceivable situation, and my favourite recollection from those times is of our stopping together during the almost vertical climb out of a Kimberley gorge—each with an enormous pack on his back—while Richard photographed an exquisite yellow native hibiscus growing from a cleft in the rocks . . . I had to turn the flower to the camera while holding on to the slope with my teeth.

Whether he is photographing a scene, an action, an abstract or an object—whether it is for himself, or a friend, or a government department or some overseas journal, or one of his own splendid publica-tions—every click of the shutter is preceded by every ounce of preparation, imagination and technical expertise he is capable of . . . and in every department mentioned, that is plenty.

Richard Woldendorp is a complete professional who has the approach, and above all, the sensibilities, of an artist. I believe Western Australia is fortunate in that this book has been produced to show the rest of Australia now, and future generations wherever it might be sold, just how we look, and act, and work, and play, and build, and dream . . . one-hundred-and-fifty years after our wonderful State was founded.

T. A. G. Hungerford

Right: Aerial view of the heart of Perth.

Two views of Perth from Kings Park. This fast-growing capital of Western Australia is the most isolated city in the world. Singapore is nearer than Sydney.

Page 6, above left: View from Applecross towards Perth on a Sunday afternoon.

Lower left: A glimpse of new and old at St. George's Tce.

Above right: The Perth Concert Hall

Lower right: A fine example of early Perth architecture at St. George's Tce.

7

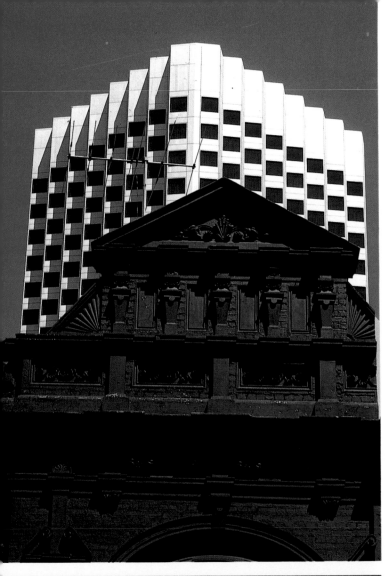

Above: Architecture, the new structures tower over buildings of earlier days.

The city centre, reflected in the broad reaches of the Swan River.

Page 10: Looking up the Swan River from Fremantle.

Page 11: Thanks to Fremantle City Council's policy of preserving and maintaining the historic character of Fremantle, the old markets are once more in full swing.

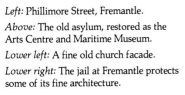

Left: Phillimore Street, Fremantle.

Above: The old asylum, restored as the Arts Centre and Maritime Museum.

Lower left: A fine old church facade.

Lower right: The jail at Fremantle protects some of its fine architecture.

History
150 years of rapid growth
Geoffrey Bolton

Western Australia's history is largely the story of efforts to overcome the handicap of isolation. Given a bad name by early Dutch navigators, avoided by the British until occupied for strategic reasons, the land disappointed the expectations of the first colonists who arrived with Captain Stirling in 1829. Remote from markets, the colony failed to attract settlers and investors, and owed its progress mainly to the convict labour introduced after 1850. It took the grant of self-government and the discovery of gold to trigger the boom of the 1890s. A great leap forward in wealth and population primed Sir John Forrest's ambitious developmental schemes and laid the foundations for the opening of the wheat-belt between 1905 and 1930. Although Western Australia was a foundation member of the Australian Commonwealth in 1901, federation was thought to have stunted its industrial growth, so that a crisis such as the depression of the 1930s evoked a strong but short-lived secession movement. Integrated more closely with the rest of Australia by the Second World War, Western Australia enjoyed three decades of postwar prosperity based on a greater diversification of industry and a massive development of mining after 1960.

This plaque, outside the R & I Bank in
Barrack Street, tells its own story.

For a big country with a keen sense of pride, Western Australia has a singularly unimaginative name. It might have been 'Hesperia', the land looking west, as suggested by Sir James Stirling, the first governor. It was 'New Holland' for the Dutch navigators of the 17th century who were the first discoverers of whom we have record; and perhaps it was the 'Java le Grande' of the Portuguese a century earlier. We do not know the names used by the first comers, the Aborigines, whose occupancy of the western part of Australia goes back much longer: at least 30,000 years, a thousand generations. With the possible exceptions of China and East Africa no part of the earth's surface is known to have been peopled longer by *Homo sapiens*.

Until recently, because they were few in number and lacking in material wealth, the Aborigines were thought to have left little impact on the face of the country they inhabited. In fact, as elsewhere in Australia, the landscape was profoundly altered by the Aboriginal custom of burning off the country year after year as an aid to hunting. These man-made fires created the good grasslands of the Kimberleys and the open park-like forest country which would prove so attractive to British settlers in the 19th century. But the sandy coastal country looked far less inviting, and it was this that provoked the first unfavourable European reactions.

From early in the 17th century Dutch navigators plying to Indonesia for spices and other valuables found that they could shorten the crossing of the Indian Ocean by catching the Roaring Forties and tacking north in the longitude of Java. Though superb seamen they were at the mercy of defective charts and under-developed navigational instruments. Some fell foul of the little-known shores of what is now Western Australia. Dirk Hartog, sighting the western tip of the continent in October 1616, sent a landing party ashore and left a pewter dinner plate on the island which bears his name. Others were less fortunate. The English ship *Tryal* was lost near the Monte Bello Islands in 1622. Seven years later Captain Pelsaert's *Batavia*, pride of the

Dutch East India Company, was wrecked in the Abrolhos. Survivors got safely ashore only to figure in a dark and bloody melodrama when mutineers planning to form a bizarre commune slaughtered those who would not join them. Pelsaert arrived with a rescue boat just in time to save the surviving loyalists and punish the wrongdoers. Several were tortured and executed, but two were marooned on the mainland to become the first white men in Western Australia. Following this episode the Dutch soon charted the northern and western shores of the continent, but during the next hundred years the coast claimed many wrecks. Since there were no prospects of trade, the Dutch formed a poor opinion of the country. This was shared by the English buccaneer, William Dampier, who damned the heat and the flies and called the Aborigines "the miserablest people on the whole earth".

Bearing such a reputation, Western Australia was not wanted when the British decided in 1788 to found a settlement on the other side of Australia. Instead, the continent west of 129°E was left unannexed for another forty years. During that time several French expeditions examined the coast; the west might easily have become Australia's equivalent of Quebec. But eventually the activities of French explorers and American whalers aroused the British government. In December 1826 Major Lockyer with a small party of soldiers and convicts was sent from New South Wales to plant the Union Jack at the magnificent harbour of King George's Sound, now the site of Albany. Two months later the enquiring and optimistic Captain James Stirling took an expedition up the Swan River which was to lead to the foundation of the colony of Western Australia.

On dangerously slender evidence Stirling was strongly impressed with the fertility and potential of the Swan valley. His glowing reports reached an England midway through a period of prolonged rural depression. The response was immediate. Retired naval and military officers, younger sons of gentry families, substantial merchants and yeoman farmers were swept into a "Swan River mania" which prompted them to invest their all in what promised to be a second New South Wales, but free of the convict taint. Among major investors Thomas Peel, cousin of the statesman Sir Robert Peel, was pre-eminent. Understanding that the venture would cost little public money, the British government created a new colony with Stirling as first governor. He arrived at the Swan River with the first white settlers in June 1829.

Disillusion soon followed. No preparations had been made for the arrival of settlers. No shelter was provided against the rainy Western Australian winter. It was two months before a site was selected for the main town, Perth, appropriately founded by the cutting down of a tree, the first of very many. No land had been allocated. The able and level-headed surveyor-general, John Septimus Roe, worked hard to sort out conflicting claims, but from want of skilled labour and ignorance of the country, the colonists were slow to move into productivity. Many, such as Thomas Peel, lapsed into despair and inertia. Had it not been for the discovery of good land in the Avon Valley beyond the Darling Range, the colony might have been abandoned. As it was, by 1832 of 4,000 arrivals in Western Australia only 1,500 remained, most of the rest having moved to Sydney or Hobart. For the next half-century Western Australia would be one of the most isolated, impoverished, and insignificant corners of the British Empire.

Isolation was the overwhelming fact of life in Western Australia. When the Round House at Fremantle was erected in 1831 it was the only significant building between Java and Tasmania. The oceans and the Nullarbor Plain are formidable barriers. Perth is still the most isolated city in the world. The approaches to the Swan River Colony in the 19th century were just as hazardous as they had been for the Dutch two centuries earlier. Fremantle was a poor harbour, and the seas around it were a sailors' graveyard. Until 1900 most shipping preferred to go to Albany, nearly 500 kilometres from Perth over indifferent roads. This shipping was the only means of communication with the outside world until the completion of a telegraph link in 1877. The construction of a railway to eastern Australia was not seriously considered until the 1880s, and not completed until 1917. It has taken the recent development of aviation to improve Western Australia's accessibility, and even now costs are high and distances long. Small wonder that Western Australians soon fostered that acute awareness of isolation which led them to see themselves as the Cinderella of Australia.

Because of its smallness and isolation Western Australia was doomed to economic stagnation during its first fifty years. Too small a local market to generate economic activity, too far behind its thriving competitors in eastern Australia to attract migrants and investment, disadvantaged after 1831 by Colonial Office regulations forbidding free or inexpensive land grants, the West was destined to haul itself painfully into solvency by its own boot-straps—unless a windfall came from some outside investor. An illusory hope was raised between 1839 and 1841 when a group of British speculators, eager to try E. G. Wakefield's theories of systematic colonization, planned a settlement at Australind, 150 kilometres south of Fremantle, where a model township would serve as port for Indian Ocean trade. Before the township was more than a plan on paper, the investors lost confidence, but at least their scheme resulted in the addition of a few hundred migrants to the colony. Otherwise the colony struggled on during the 1840s in poverty, its export income coming from a little whaling, a little woolgrowing, and the opening of a market in sandalwood with China after 1845. Twenty years after Stirling's expedition the Swan River Colony supported only about 5,000 inhabitants. There were probably at least as many Aborigines in the South-West before the arrival of what called itself European civilization.

The Aborigines were already a defeated race. During the first few years of white settlement they offered sporadic resistance. One leader, Yagan of the Bibbulmun, made a considerable reputation before he was shot by a white youth whom he thought his friend, and his head was sent to Britain as an anthropological curiosity. Diphtheria, measles, and other newly introduced epidemics did more to lessen their numbers than racial conflict. Soon the Aborigines of the South-West adapted themselves to a role as fringe-dwellers in society. Considerable effort was devoted to their education by the Wesleyan missionary Smithies and the Spanish Benedictine bishop, Rosendo Salvado, who arrived in 1846. Founder and for more than fifty years abbot of the New Norcia mission, Salvado became one of the folk heroes of Western Australia with his mixture of aristocratic culture, humane charity, and shrewd acquisitiveness on behalf of the mission. But by the time he died in 1900 many of the Aboriginal tribes of the South-West were close to extinction.

Since the Aborigines were not readily available for Western Australia's labour force, alternatives were sought. By 1850 it was evident that the only likely source of cheap labour would come from the introduction of British convicts. This was a bitter pill for Western Australia, especially as the other Australian colonies were self-righteously abandoning convict labour and hastening towards self-government. The decision nevertheless triggered the colony's first stage of significant economic growth. Between 1850 and 1868 nearly 10,000 convicts arrived in Western Australia. During that time the population quadrupled, wool exports increased fivefold, the colony's first major roads were constructed, and Perth and Fremantle acquired their first substantial buildings, such as the Perth Town Hall and the Fremantle Museum (originally an asylum). The investment of British government money in the convict establishment did much to stimulate local trade, especially in providing a market for farmers and a nucleus of workers for pastoralists. The Geraldton district went ahead in the 1850s, and following F. T. Gregory's expedition to the North-West in 1861 several pioneering parties established sheep-runs in the country around Roe-

bourne. Prosperity came to them slowly, and several eked out their resources by pearling with Aboriginal labour. Two Victorian-based enterprises sought to establish pastoral settlements at Camden Harbour and Roebuck Bay in 1864, but were repelled by hostile Aborigines and harsh conditions. Despite these setbacks, Western Australia had laid firm foundations for future growth by the time convict transportation ceased in 1868.

Looking at the inspiring examples of Victoria and New South Wales, Western Australians now hoped for a goldrush to take them further on the road to wealth and progress. Unfortunately "expert" opinion insisted that there was no gold in Western Australia. The 1870s saw economic recession, especially for the farmers. On other fronts growth continued modestly. Between 1870 and 1879 the Forrest brothers led several major inland expeditions, twice traversing the desert between Western and South Australia, and opening the Fitzroy and Ord valleys in the Kimberleys. A mainly elected Legislative Council was set up in 1870, under whose auspices the colony was linked to eastern Australia by telegraph and the first railways completed—from Geraldton to Northampton in 1879, from Fremantle to Guildford in 1881 and then to York in 1886. Early in the 1880s several groups of outside capitalists sought concessions to build major railway lines in return for large grants of land along their routes. Two schemes were authorized, one linking Perth with Albany (completed in 1889) and the other to Geraldton. Unfortunately after providing an initial boost to the colony's economy both companies fell into difficulties, but their activity at least signalled that the outside world was belatedly taking an interest in Western Australia. In the far north the advance of the pastoral frontier from Queensland brought the Duracks, the Macdonalds, and several parties of overlanding cattlemen into the East Kimberley district in 1883-85. The stage was set for Western Australia's first major period of boom.

Prospectors followed the overlanders. A small discovery of gold at Hall's Creek in the Kimberleys

17

stimulated Western Australia's first gold-rush in 1886. Though it proved short-lived, the rush triggered other finds in the Pilbara and Yilgarn districts (1887-8). From these it was a short step to the much bigger discoveries at the Murchison (1891), Coolgardie (1892), and Kalgoorlie (1893). Even before these later finds a new-found confidence in their future led Western Australians to agitate for self-government. Because of the rather contentious tone of Perth politics in the 1880s the British government was reluctant to entrust the 46,000 inhabitants of Western Australia with the responsibility for running nearly a million square miles, but eventually conceded it in 1890. The respected, locally-born explorer and surveyor, Sir John Forrest, became the colony's first premier. Contrary to the experience of other Australian colonies, Western Australia's first ministry proved unusually stable. Forrest dominated the colony's politics for over ten years, retiring in 1901 only to enter the federal sphere. His success was due mainly to his own prestige, judgment, and political astuteness, but he also had great good luck with his timing.

The news of Coolgardie and Kalgoorlie reached an eastern Australia sliding into its worst depression for fifty years. Migrants flocked to the diggings, mainly from Victoria and South Australia. Between 1890 to 1904 Western Australia's population rose by over 500 percent, to 239,000. British capitalists, eagerly seeking outlets for mining investment, bought heavily into the Golden Mile and other fields. All too often they burned their fingers, but the spin-off for Western Australia was valuable. Ably served by the engineer C. Y. O'Connor, the Forrest government hastened to service the goldfields by building railways to Southern Cross, Kalgoorlie, and Cue almost before the permanence of their gold was established. To bring water to the arid eastern goldfields O'Connor planned a pipeline from Mundaring 550 kilometres in length. The longest in the world, it was completed in January 1903, but by that time O'Connor was driven to suicide by incessant partisan criticism of what was thought an impossible scheme. O'Connor's other great work was the construction of an artificial harbour at Fremantle during the 1890s, another task previously defying expert opinion. It took a lavish outlay of capital, available only because of boom conditions. It led to stagnation for outports such as Albany, Esperance, and Geraldton. The Forrest government deliberately centralized the colony's transport system on Perth and Fremantle, and thus permanently confirmed the metropolitan region as by far the biggest concentration of population in Western Australia. At the time the policy could be justified as a wise use of public resources, but it was to lead to the lack of balance between town and country which is today even more marked in the West than in any other Australian State.

The newcomers to the goldfields resented the domination of Perth. Schooled in the tougher and more radical politics of Melbourne and Sydney, they derided the countryfied conservatism of the old 'sandgroper' families, and demanded parliamentary reform and lower tariffs on food—thus, of course, coming into conflict with farming interests. There was also some resentment of mining legislation which tended to favour investors over working miners. Forrest fenced tenaciously with this growing opposition, conceding a point here, buying off critics with a new railway or public building there. By 1899 goldfields spokesmen had a powerful weapon in the federation movement. Themselves recent comers from the East, they threatened to work for a secession movement which would unite the goldfields to the rest of the Australian Commonwealth and leave the West devoid of its new-found wealth. Forrest hedged, even introducing votes for women as a counter to the largely masculine goldfields. He bargained cannily with the representatives of other Australian colonies, securing the promise of a staging-out period for Western Australian tariffs and a commitment to the building of a transcontinental railway. Even so, he could not carry many of his own followers into giving up their opposition to federation. The 'sandgroper'-dominated Legislative Council at first threw out his proposals for a referendum on the issue. Following pressure from the British government the poll was held in mid-1900, and resulted in a "yes" vote for federation by 44,000 votes to 19,000; but many of the older colonists were unhappy with the result.

Sir John Forrest's departure into federal politics left a vacuum in Western Australian politics. A few years of political instability followed. The Labor movement gained ground rapidly among goldfields and coastal workers, but when in 1904-05 a minority Labor government took office its opponents soon sank their differences and coalesced to overthrow it. These years of instability coincided with the end of the boom of the nineties. The production of gold peaked in 1903 and then began a quarter-century of slow decline which was to leave many formerly thriving communities empty and derelict. Of the State's other industries, timber continued to thrive following the boom, and a prosperous pearling industry was at its zenith at Broome. Established around 1886, pearling at Broome provided the West with its major multiracial community to survive the coming of the White Australia policy. In order to ensure the survival of the industry the authorities winked at the presence of numerous Japanese, Indonesian, and Malayan divers and crewmen. Pearling and timber alone could not compensate for the downturn in mining. For continued prosperity Western Australia needed to develop other staples. Such infant manufacturing industries as had managed to get a start were hit hard by federation and the removal of tariff protection, and many succumbed to Eastern States competition. This caused enough disquiet to persuade the State Parliament in 1906 to pass a resolution in favour of secession from the Commonwealth, but nothing came of it. Instead the State's politicians devoted themselves wholeheartedly to the promotion of Western Australia's major hope for the future: wheatgrowing.

Ever optimistic about the future of the West, Forrest in his time laid the foundations for a wheatgrowing industry by legislating for cheap land and set-

ting up in 1895 an Agricultural Bank (now the Rural and Industries Bank) with the specific responsibility of making credit available to farmers on easy terms. Again he was lucky in his timing. Within the next few years William Farrer perfected the varieties of 'dry' wheat which would allow for the inland expansion of Australia's wheatgrowing zones, and superphosphate replaced guano as a cheaper and more efficient means of fertilization. By 1905 conditions were ripe for a push forward. Newton Moore, Premier 1906-10, and his lieutenant, James Mitchell were both disciples of Forrest and promoted his policies zealously. Within five years the frontier of wheatgrowing advanced by 250 kilometres. Many of the new farmers were ex-miners: 'Gold brought these men here', said Mitchell, 'and superphosphate will keep them here'. Other settlers included younger sons from the crowded farmlands of South Australia, British migrants in quest of a more spacious future, and a surprising number of established city businessmen attracted by rural life. To Western Australians of that generation it was an article of faith that city life was in many ways inferior to the healthier and more genuinely productive life of the country-dweller. Politicians saw it as their task to get people out of the towns; James Mitchell to the end of his long life exhorted young men to go on the land and young women to become farmers' wives and have numerous children. The governments of the day threw most of their energies into an orgy of country railway-building and the provision of other rural amenities. Far less attention was given to the provision of city requirements and almost none to industrialization.

In those circumstances the most important trade unions became those servicing transport: the wharf labourers, the railwaymen, and the coal-miners of Collie (a low-grade deposit worked since 1898 mainly to service the State's expanding railways). On their own they could not have created a strong Labor movement, but they were reinforced by workers in the pastoral and goldmining industries. As population dwindled in the goldfields Labor came to dominate the outback, and in 1911 enjoyed a landslide victory. The new Premier, Scaddan, earned the nickname 'Gone-a-million Jack' for the public money lost during the next few years on various experiments in State ownership. Most of these were founded not on a doctrinaire obsession with socialism, but from a desire to provide competition with retailers whose prices were thought to be excessive. But the State bakeries and butcheries proved inefficient and soon went out of business, and the one legacy of all this activity was the State Shipping Service to North-West ports. Scaddan's term of office coincided with two bad droughts in 1911 and 1914. These forced many of the new wheat-belt farmers off the land, and produced a discontent which led to the appearance of Australia's first successful Country party in 1914. This group held the balance of power in the Legislative Assembly, and in 1916 turned Labor out of Office to support the Liberals.

The First World War cut across the drought and political problems. No part of Australia rallied more fervently to the cause of the British Empire than Western Australia. It offered a higher percentage of voluntary recruits for the armed forces, a more generous financial contribution to patriotic funds, and a stronger vote in favour of military conscription than any other part of the Commonwealth. The Labor party was reluctant to make conscription a matter to split over, and did so only after insistent urging from its colleagues in the Eastern States. This strong sense of patriotic unity lasted until the coming of peace in November 1918, but reaction soon followed. The problems of assimilating hundreds of weary and war-shocked ex-servicemen were exacerbated by a severe epidemic of "Spanish" influenza which claimed a number of lives. An unusual outbreak of trade union militancy culminated in a waterfront strike in May 1919 in which one man was shot dead and a bag of old iron hurled at the State Premier of the day. Soon, however, Western Australia recovered its sense of stable con-census. Politics were dominated between the two

world wars by the Nationalist leader Sir James Mitchell and Labor's Philip Collier, whose differences of opinion were about tactics rather than long-term goals for the State.

Satisfied that the wheatgrowing industry was recovering and advancing, Mitchell turned his energies to promoting dairy-farming in the South-West. He zealously promoted a scheme for 'group settlements'. These were co-operatives in which recent British migrants were to band together to clear the land and prepare blocks of country which would be allocated to them individually, after they gained experience of rural life. The scheme met with early enthusiasm, but was largely a failure. Many of the migrants were inexperienced in bush life, and after trying to grapple with hardship and isolation, quit in despair. Those who remained often found that the land was too poor, since the role of trace elements had not yet been discovered. The scheme was maintained by Philip Collier's Labor government, but without markedly greater success. An irony of the 1920s was that the continual efforts of governments to attract settlers to the country resulted only in the steady growth of Perth's suburbs. For most inhabitants of Western Australia, indeed, the decade was one of increasing material comfort. The use of telephones and motor-cars was becoming more common. Aviation was beginning to link the West with the rest of Australia. A service operated to the North-West from 1921, initiated by Major (now Sir) Norman Brearley with help from, among others, Kingsford-Smith; and in 1929 the first regular air service was established between Perth and the Eastern States. By 1929 Western Australia could celebrate its centenary with a considerable sense of pride in achievement.

This achievement was precariously based on the continuation of good export prices for wheat and wool. The world depression of 1929-33, while it came later to Western Australia than to the rest of the continent, struck with savage severity. Mitchell, again Premier 1930-33, exhorted farmers to beat falling prices by producing more, but despite a record harvest in 1930 of over 53 million bushels (never to be exceeded for over thirty years), the slump in markets left primary producers in grave trouble. Many farmers found it impossible to make ends meet, and in the end were obliged simply to walk off the land. Others survived only by paring their expenses to the bone. Boiled wheat, treacle, and rabbit became their main items of diet. In many cases farmers were permitted to stay on their farms only by pledging their entire takings to the control of their creditors. Many more survived only through the leniency of storekeepers, themselves hard-pressed. The number of city unemployed also soared. By 1932 an estimated 30 per cent of trade unionists were out of work, to say nothing of the hardships faced by self-employed artisans and tradesmen. Many of them were sent to bush camps and placed on sustenance work clearing timber and labouring on irrigation projects.

Anger and frustration led during 1931-32 to a number of demonstrations in Perth, most of them easily dispersed by police. The farmers, too, banded themselves into a wheatgrowers' union which threatened to withhold the harvest of 1932, but the 'strike' collapsed after a fortnight when it was seen to command only partial support. Strongest reaction of all to the depression was a sudden uprush of support for the secession movement, fed by tariff grievances and remoteness from the costly new national capital at Canberra. At a referendum held in April 1933 nearly 70 per cent of the voters said 'Yes' to secession. But simultaneously the secessionist Mitchell was swept from office, and his old rival Collier returned to initiate fourteen years of Labor government. Magnanimously Collier made Mitchell lieutenant-governor, a role he filled with distinction until just before his death in 1951. Playing for time, Collier managed to delay the submission of the secession petition to the British Parliament until 1935. The House of Commons refused to intervene, and by this time the fire had gone out of the secession movement. Recovery from the depression was led by the goldmining industry, which absorbed many

of the unemployed, though not without an outbreak of anti-foreign rioting at Kalgoorlie in January 1934. Probably the most spectacular figure in mining at that time was the promoter Claude de Bernales, as notable for the creation of Perth's sham-Tudor London Court as for the skill with which he enticed capital from British investors. Despite the boom in goldmining and a modest revival in the dairy industry, the wheat farmers remained in dire straits until the Second World War, and the pastoralists' recovery. Already subsidising such claimant States North-West between 1935 and 1940. The Commonwealth government played its part in assisting recovery. Already subsidising such claimant states as Western Australia, it was jogged by the secession movement into setting up a Grants Commission to extend this aid.

It took the Second World War of 1939-45 to knit the West firmly into the Australian community. As in the First World War, Western Australia contributed generously to the war effort, particularly after the entry of Japan into the war at the end of 1941. During the following critical months many refugees from Malaya and Indonesia found their way to Western Australia. The North-West ports of Broome and Wyndham were bombed. Preparations were made against air-raids, and many feared a Japanese invasion. The Australian war effort which eventually averted this threat was led by the only prime minister ever to come from a Western Australian constituency, John Curtin. Out of this war effort came the first significant beginnings of industrialization in Western Australia, as well as an extension of the benefits of Commonwealth social services. On the other hand State rights were considerably eroded, and uniform taxation and other centralizations of power in Canberra were accepted only under protest. The work of integration continued in a variety of ways after the end of the war in 1945. The growth of interstate travel was fostered in 1946 when a second airline linked Perth with eastern capitals. To many it mattered more that Western Australia was admitted to the interstate Sheffield Shield cricket tournament in 1948—and won in the same year.

Post war prosperity was buoyed up by a continued demand for wheat, wool, and dairy produce. Under the guidance of the engineer-administrator Sir Russell Dumas a strong drive was made for diversification. Partial success was reached in 1952 when investors agreed to build an oil refinery and steel rolling mill in the new Kwinana industrial area on Cockburn Sound. Oil was discovered at Exmouth Gulf in 1953, to the intense excitement of the stock exchange, but without permanent result. With the application of trace elements to previously unsuitable land it became possible to resume the advance of the marginal wheatlands, and by 1960 the harvest exceeded the record of 1930. Attempts were made, not always with happy consequences, to attract American investors in primary production in the Esperance district.

It took the mineral boom of the 1960s to stimulate an impressive flow of foreign capital to Western Australia. Before 1960 the only exploitation of iron ore in the State was at Koolan Island in the Kimberleys. Once the embargo on iron ore exports was lifted in that year it was not long before several rich deposits were located in the Pilbara. The most notable among the developers was the pastoralist Lang Hancock, already connected with the asbestos industry of the North-West at Wittenoom; a hard-driving individual whose forceful views on mineral policy frequently brought him into conflict with State and federal governments, he was eventually to attempt almost single-handed the revival of the secession movement. The main responsibility for managing mineral development lay with the Liberal-Country party government of Sir David Brand (Premier, 1959-71) and his energetic colleague Sir Charles Court (Premier since 1974). Major American, Japanese, and British companies were persuaded to undertake substantial investment in the Pilbara, constructing several new railways and towns, and establishing an important export trade in iron ore, largely with Japan. Substantial deposits of nickel, bauxite, ilmenite, and uranium were also found and in many cases

developed for export. A more contentious exercise in northern development was the damming of the Ord river for growing sugar, cotton, and other forms of tropical agriculture. Few of the farmers enjoyed great success, and the ecological consequences of the scheme came under close scrutiny.

In the main, however, the record of Western Australia's economic development since 1945 was a success story. Even when recession came in the 1970s its impact was much softer in Western Australia than elsewhere in the Commonwealth. In thirty years since the Second World War the State's population grew from half a million to over 1.1 million. Over two-thirds were concentrated in the Perth metropolitan area. Although concern was often expressed about the problems of urbanization and environmental control, most industrial and commercial development was centred on the metropolis, and experts could see no limit to the growth of Perth. As Perth prepared to celebrate its 150th birthday in 1979, its beauty was still largely unimpaired by its growth from being an overgrown country town to a thriving city. It was by now a far cry from the shabby-genteel penury of the first British settlers, eking out an existence on slender resources. The problems which now confronted Western Australia were largely those resulting from affluence. Only the isolation remained a constant factor; and if it made for a certain amount of complacency and provincialism, it also produced a community with a distinctive character, a reasonable degree of practical tolerance, and a rare sense of hopefulness that the chance still remained to avoid some of the mistakes and problems of older and bigger societies.

Right: Named Rats' Nest by the early Dutch explorers who didn't know a quokka when they saw one, Rottnest was settled from the earliest days, and is still popular as a holiday island for metropolitan Perth.

Above left: All Saints Church, Upper Swan: the oldest church in Western Australia.

Lower left: Tranby-on-Swan, on the edge of the Swan River, near Maylands.

Above; Woodbridge, further up the Swan River at Guildford. Restored by the National Trust.

The old church at Guildford.

Far left: York, one of the earliest farming towns, 100 kms east of Perth. Its annual arts & crafts festival attracts thousands of visitors to enjoy its old-world charm.

Toodyay, an important farming community 100 km east of Perth, with an interesting historical background.

New Norcia, 131 km north of Perth on the
Gt. Northern Highway. Founded in 1846
by a Spanish monk, Don Rosendo Salvado,
of the Benedictine Order.

Far left above: Traditional Australian farmhouse near Busselton.

Above left: Steam engines, like the Lady Leschenaultia, are running once again, as a tourist attraction, thanks to local enthusiasts, and help from the West Australian Government Railways.

Far left lower: Through the leaded pane: the altar of St. Mark's, Picton, the oldest church in the district.

Above right: Fossilized water wheel on the coast at Augusta.

Left: The Blechyndon House on the Blackwood River, restored by the National Trust.

31

Albany, with its magnificent harbour, was settled before Perth, and boasts some fine architecture from the early days.

Above right: Strawberry Hill Farm.

Elegant early homes.

Middle right: The Scots Presbyterian Church, in the main street of Albany.

Far right: The Anzac Memorial.

A contestant in the Perth to Albany yacht race contrasts with a replica of the Brig *Amity*.

Far right above: Pelicans in Princess Harbour. A telephoto view across to Albany.

Far right lower: Ravensthorpe, an early mining town east of Albany.

Page 36, above left: Shades of the old goldmining days of Norseman.

Lower left: Esperance, historic homestead

Right-hand page: The Gold Fields. Now only traces remain of the booming gold-rush days.

Above: Poppet Heads standing idle along
the golden mile at Kalgoorlie, once one
of the richest deposits in the world.

Above: Main street, Boulder.

As gold mining died out, other minerals of value to world markets were found, so that Kalgoorlie has kept its importance as the regional centre of the new mining areas.

Top left: Housing in the new nickel mining town of Kambalda.

Middle left: Kalgoorlie supermarket.

Lower left: Kambalda shopping centre.

Kalgoorlie shoppers.

Above and lower left: Hannan Street, Kalgoorlie: the main street, named after Paddy Hannan, who first discovered gold in Kalgoorlie.

Above centre: The Afghan camel drivers left their mark on the Kalgoorlie scene.

Above right: Kalgoorlie reflected in one of its many pubs.

Above, lower left: Cue, North of Kalgoorlie:
many beautiful buildings still stand in this
old gold-mining town.

Lower right: Old jail, near Mount Gould.

Cue, an architectural gem in corrugated iron.

Left: This hand-made gold battery, still stands at Meekatharra.

Above left: Before the pipeline was built, water shortage was the main problem in the goldfields. This low stone structure channelled any rainwater into a natural reservoir.

Above right: The slag heap creeps up on the old acid vats of Daydawn.

Above: Greenough Flats: until mechanization put small farms out of business, an early community worked the rich coastal plain between Dongara and Geraldton.

Lower left: Modern farm, Greenough.

Lower right: The old flour mill, Dongara.

Above: Greenough church, inside and out.

Above left: Cannon from the wrecks of the early Dutch explorers, came from the Abrolhos, now displayed in Geraldton.

Lower left: Fishing boats in the Geraldton harbour.

Right-hand page: Carnarvon, coastal town, and stepping stone to the North West.

49

Pioneer's grave.

Japanese divers' cemetery.

Above right: Steps from the courthouse to the main jetty at Cossack, once the biggest port in the North West.

Above right: Chinatown, Broome, once a melting pot for all the races of the world.

Lower left: An annual lugger race still marks the end of the pearling season at Broome, old capital of the pearling world.

Argyll homestead, home of the Durack
family, moved to its present location near
the Ord dam, when its old site was flooded

Aerial view of Thomson's Bay, Rottnest Island.

Australians have often been written off as suburbanites,
but they have the best of both worlds—
a low rise, urban lifestyle, with plenty of space around their cities
to escape to on holidays or weekends.
In a hot, dry continent, water particularly attracts them,
and their cities cling to the river and ocean fronts.

One of the attractions of Rottnest are the quokkas.

55

Rottnest lighthouse, across Herschell Lake.

Surfing.

Fishing off the North Mole, Fremantle in
the background.

Lifesavers preparing for a race.

Many people soak up the sun on our fine metropolitan beaches.

There are so many things for children to do.

Above left: Festival of Perth.

Above right: Chess at Kalamunda.

Lower left: Building a pyramid on the
Canning River.

Lower right: A children's play at the
Concert Hall.

Canoeing has become popular in recent years.
The Avon descent.
Lower left: The tranquil Blackwood.
Right: The Murchison River at Kalbarri.

Above: Pearl auction at Broome.
Prince Leonard.
Kings Park adventure playground.
Beagle Bay Mission artist.

The picnic.

Social
People at work and play
Kirwan Ward

The million or so West Australians, though they occupy one third of the Australian continent, make up only about one eighth of Australia's population. This spaciousness, this situation of one free-breathing West Australian to heaven-knows-how-many hectares of land has gradually produced, over nearly a century-and-a-half, an Australian citizen with a subdued but definite sense of elitism, rather like the attitude of a Texan to the rest of the United States of America.

In spite of the fact that "boom" is a dirty word in Harvest Terrace, where State Parliament sits, the State's progress has undeniably been in a series of massive, kangaroo hops rather than by a gentle progression of sedate steps. First of all it was gold, at Coolgardie, Kalgoorlie and in the world-famous Golden Mile; then wheat, then wool, then oil, then nickel, iron ore, and bauxite, and seemingly limitless quantities of natural gas. Beyond all this, these days in a world that must soon plainly turn to solar energy, is the thought that inexhaustible sunshine is as dependable in the West as it is anywhere on this planet.

From this favoured environment, rugged though it has been, has evolved an independently-minded citizen, now accustomed, as of right of heritage, to a high standard of living and leisure. The old picture of West Australians, widely held in Eastern States, was of shabby Cinderellas enviously watching their elder and wealthier sisters preparing for the ball. It may have been valid years ago when the only link with the Federal seat of government was a once-a-week train of doubtful performance, a transcontinental road that was an adventurous gravel track, or an occasional steamer rolling through the Bight. Not now.

Now, if the ordinary West Australian has any belief in anything, and no matter how much he may indulge in traditional grumbles, it is the belief that he is, by geographical chance, one of the luckiest people on earth.

People of the West.

White settlement in Western Australia began on June 2 1829 when 44 adults, two youths, 14 children and eight infants arrived, in the transport *Parmelia*, to settle in what had been known as New Holland, and what was to become, in a few days, the Swan River Colony. They had sailed half-way round the world, from Spithead, England, in a ship smaller than one of today's Rottnest ferries, expecting to find a lush promised land of perpetual sunshine. Instead they gazed with dismay through winter squalls at a featureless shoreline, bleak as a lunar landscape, lashed by bone-chilling winds that screamed up from the south.

The *Parmelia's* "Pilgrim Fathers" were all British middle-class professional people, or skilled tradesmen, free settlers all, without a convicted person among them. Men and women of brave, adventurous character and ability, surgeons, surveyors, master mariners, an agriculturalist, a boat builder, a storekeeper . . . surely no new colony was ever built upon a sounder human foundation.

In fact, Western Australia was never a penal colony in the sense that some other Australian States were, and convicts were not introduced until 1850, 21 years after the founding of the colony, when a desperate shortage of manpower for the roads, bridges, and buildings forced a bare, reluctant majority to petition the Colonial Office in London for selected good behaviour prisoners. As with the garrison soldiers and pensioners' guard, transported convicts who had served their sentence were given the opportunity to remain in Western Australia. When the last convict ship, the *Hougemont* discharged her human cargo at Fremantle in 1868, some 9,721 convicts had been brought to W.A. during an 18-year phase, outnumbering the 6122 free settlers who had arrived in the same period.

By the time of the 1976 census, the population of Western Australia had grown, from that modest figure of 68 persons, to 1,144,857, and W.A. emerged as the nation's fastest-growing State, with a growth rate for the census of 2.13 per cent. Perth, the capital, built on the beautiful riverside site which had so attracted Captain Stirling, had become Australia's fifth biggest city, and the expectation was that, by the end of the 20th century, only 24 years away, it would be third biggest after only Sydney and Melbourne.

Strangers sometimes believe that they can detect slight differences, in speech and characteristics, between West Australians and the 12 million other Australians living so many miles to eastward. Whether such differences do actually exist is arguable, but what isn't arguable is that a distinctive life style has evolved on the western seaboard. It is the life style of a people who, for at least a century, have been cushioned by isolation against the worst of the outside world's social and economic ills. The style of a people who, in nearly 150 years of statehood, have scarcely known a natural disaster, certainly no major disaster as the world understands the term. It is the natural prosperous life style of a handful of privileged people occupying an area the size of Western Europe and one of the most mineral-rich areas on earth.

Probably the most significant factor in the moulding of the West Australian character is distance. Distance almost beyond the comprehension of Europeans, with the State's northernmost settlements sweltering in the tropics and the southernmost, 2500 kilometres away, shivering on the fringes of Antarctica. Perth is nearer to Jakarta, Indonesia than it is to Sydney, Australia; and to people in Port Hedland W.A., planning a holiday escape from the north-west heat and iron-ore dust, the beaches of Bali are much closer than those of W.A's famous Rottnest Island. There are single sheep and cattle stations in Western Australia's north that are bigger than the county of Yorkshire.

A few months ago I drove south from the Eyre Highway on the Nullarbor Plain, crossing the old "Overland" track, now only a set of parallel wheel scars beneath the creeping scrub, to the Great Australian Bight. The man who drove me over 15 km of jolting bush trail which he had hacked out, years ago, with axe and mattock, was a tough little Scot, whose native Highland accent seemed to have been sand-papered by the abrasive desert wind that nags, night and day, at the scattered settlers on the Nullarbor.

He had migrated in 1931, during doleful Depression days, and had gradually drifted eastwards almost to the South Australian border, rabbit-trapping, well-sinking, doing any work he could find. Now, as we stood ankle-deep in the white-as-talcum-powder sand of the Bight, surveying a 40 km curve of bay, he said, sweeping a casual hand around the horizon: *"That's all mine."*

It sounded wildly improbable for anyone but a wealthy squatter, but it was true. For a nominal annual fee, this little battler, whose income might not compare well with that of a city dustman, holds a grazing lease over nearly half-a-million of these arid acres.

He isn't, of course, cited as an example of the typical West Australian outback settler. He may, indeed, be one of the few men in the world, of his humble financial status, with proprietorial rights over such a huge tract of land, but his laconically-told story does illustrate both the vastness of the State itself, and the easygoing approach to life of those who live there.

Though Western Australia will, in June 1979, celebrate its 150th birthday, what the State will really be celebrating, with perhaps typical disregard for the original inhabitants, is 150 years of European settlement, for the Aborigines had preceded the "Parmelians" by possibly 10,000 years or more. Anthropologists, after examining numerous ancient skulls and artefacts, can still reach no agreement as to the source of the Australian Aborigine who, oddly enough, has never acquired a particular genetic name as have, for example, the Maoris in New Zealand. The term "Aborigine" derives from two Latin words, "ab" meaning "from", and "origine" meaning "the original". It is applicable to the original inhabitants of any country and not specifically to the Australian native.

The first European known to have observed West Australian Aborigines was Dutch explorer Dirk Hartog, in 1616, and Englishman William Dampier, who visited the North-West coast 83 years later wrote in his log that the natives he saw were "the miserablest people on the whole earth".

To Western Australian's early white settlers, the Aborigine was an enigma, an extraordinary type of prehistoric human being who simply failed to fit into any previously known human pattern. They were nomads who drifted about over the endless plains like clouds floating across the desert sky. To anyone at all familiar with such ancient peoples of civilisation as the Incas and the Egyptians, the Australian native was a mystery. He showed no interest in accumulating worldly goods, other than the most primitive of weapons and tools; he stored no food; he had seemingly no concept of comfort, was totally improvident and lived, not merely from day to day, but from meal to meal. He made not the slightest attempt at agriculture, raised no flocks, and gave no thought at all to husbandry. He built no buildings, never surrounded himself with walls or compounds, never built a ship, and never even bothered to establish a village.

It would be impertinent in so short and so cursory an essay as this to try to discuss the enormous, in-built problems of absorbing the Aborigine into any white community, but it is, rightly, a matter that continually occupies the attention of all Australian governments. In this context it may be worth recording the comment of the Australian Encyclopaedia upon the attitudes of the first white settlers:

"The local policy of goodwill towards the Aborigines was much more definite in the West than it was in the eastern colonies . . ."

The West Australian Aborigines, though never to be seriously compared as an effective workforce with, say, the cotton slaves of early America, with the sugar cane workers of the West Indies, or with the gold and diamond miners of South Africa, gradually found a niche here and there in the incomprehensible new society that was growing up around them.

Sheep and cattle stations (known in other

countries as ranches) established an easy-going, give and take sort of feudal system. Almost entire tribes would settle on a station where some members of the tribe might work, happily ceding all responsibility for their own welfare to the squatter who became such a patriarchal figure that many took his name.

The one sphere in which the West Australian Aborigine, as well as the Northern Territory Aborigine, became a specialist often superior to the white man, was as stockman or drover; a horseman, that is, to muster sheep and cattle and drive them over enormous distances to agistment or market. Although, until the coming of the white man, a horse would have been at least as curious a creature as a dinosaur, the Aborigine quickly became a notable horseman. The traveller who travels far enough north, and gets far enough away from the main roads, can still sometimes see slim, dark horseman, faces shaded by wide sombreros, riding silently through the bush, while the herd wanders ahead, scuffling up the dust into low pink clouds that hang among the scrawny undergrowth. These days, though, it is more common to see Aborigines racing round the herd on motor cycles, like trail bike riders, in contact by two-way radio with a spotter aircraft overhead.

The pioneers, from 1829 onwards, often found it possible to establish reasonably friendly relations with these mysterious Stone Age tribes to whom white people must have been a sight more astonishing than the Martians would be today were they to come hovercrafting up the Swan in echelon. But the relationship was always precarious, fraught with mutual distrust and suspicion, and armed clashes were common.

The most notable enemy to the white intruders was a picturesque young warrior named Yagan, chief of a tribe whose territory took in the present Perth metropolitan area from the Darling Range to the sea and extending southward as far as Rockingham. While leading a fight against the settlers in 1831, Yagan was captured. In pursuance of the goodwill policy he was taken to Carnac Island where it was hoped that by kindness and patient education he might be taught to trust the white man and to become a liaison officer between the Old and the New Australians.

Yagan fell out with one of his guards and, though he knew very little about boats or seamanship, managed to steal a boat and escape to the mainland where he conducted running guerilla warfare. The official attitude to Yagan's harassments was still one of supernatural tolerance, but when in 1834 a young soldier of the Royal Scots Fusiliers was murdered, near Mandurah, the time had come for punitive action. Captain Sir James Stirling led an expedition into the Murray district where Yagan and his warriors were soon encountered in the vicinity of Pinjarra.

One of Stirling's officers died from spear wounds, and a constable was wounded while Yagan's party suffered 15-20 mortal casualties. This confrontation, one of the comparatively few instances of violence in the State story, came to be known as the Battle of Pinjarra.

On a later vengeance expedition, Yagan's warriors ambushed and murdered two farmers on the Canning. With a wanted-dead-or-alive tag on his head Yagan was shot dead by a young white kangaroo hunter.

In 1954 Western Australia's parliament passed a Natives Citizenship Rights Act designed to afford Aborigines opportunities to apply for full citizenship rights.

Western Australia, like the rest of Australia, is in essence, a migrant community. The "Parmelians", and all who followed them, were migrants seeking a new life in a brave new world, and it is doubtful if an Aborigine looking at a fourth generation Australian would make any significant distinction between him and any white man who had arrived by yesterday's aircraft from Europe.

The popular notion of an Australian, even within Australia itself, is of a tall, lean outbacker, sitting slack in the saddle, slitting his eyes against the fierce sunlight as he gazes across a wide, brown land. In fact, he is likely to be a man who knows more about starting a car with a flat battery than he knows about saddling a horse, for the population—and this applies to Western Australia in particular—is overwhelmingly urban. Of W.A.'s overall population of 1,144,857 quoted earlier, 805,489 live in the Perth metropolitan region while the smaller cities like Kalgoorlie, Geraldton, Bunbury, Albany and Collie account for many thousands more. In Perth, growing faster than any other Australian State capital, the ratio of persons to car—a sure pointer both to prosperity and problems—is 1.5 persons per car, one of the highest ratios in the world.

If distance and the feeling always of plenty of space, the assurance of limitless development possibilities, have shaped the West Australian character, then, surely, so has the weather. It is as if sunshine has seeped into the bones and very chromosomes of the people, including a relaxed attitude that obscures from the casual observer the soundness of the basic values.

When a West Australian, contemplating some worrying situation, drawls: "She'll be right, mate," he isn't necessarily betraying, as strangers often think he is, indolence, laissez-faire, or apathy; he is simply unconsciously expressing his optimistic outlook. Faith in the future springs as naturally from West Australian soil as do the wildflowers.

An aspect of white settlement in Western Australia which seems to have escaped notice or comment by sociologists is that though the State's founding fathers were of exactly the same type of British people who had established Britain's colonies elsewhere, they went about their colonial mission in an entirely different way. Elsewhere the pattern had been to establish immediately a master-and-servant working relationship with the indigenous inhabitants who were quickly recruited, by one means or another, as manual labourers. Here in the West, where local inhabitants tended to be as intangible as smoke drifting through the bush, the white man had to be his own hard labourer, with no job too menial for him, from the moment that

he landed and began building crude shelter for his family in the dismal sand dunes.

Here there were never any faithful amahs or ayahs, no punkah wallahs, no dhobis, no houseboys. Darkies may have worked on the Mississippi, while the white man played, as the old Showboat song said, but not here in wildest Western Australia. Here there were no convenient coolies to tackle all the tasks that were too tough or too unpleasant for the white man. Here there were no sahibs, no bwanas, no tuans. Even the convict workforce that tamed the wild land with roads and bridges and buildings was entirely Anglo-Saxon. The hard, sweaty labour of the new colony was all done, then, as now, by the white settlers, and from this unusual work ethic has derived the independence that is so significant a part of the West Australian character.

This is not to suggest that the first settlers deliberately set out to establish a classless community. In fact, they instinctively did everything they could to establish exactly the same sort of social background as they had known in the Old Country. Many of them brought personal servants with them and set up the kind of minor feudalism that you would have found, in those days, among the squireocracy in an English village. But the tough environment, the need for everyone to work to capacity as a matter of survival, and the obvious opportunities for anybody of any status, made nonsense of class pretensions.

Of course, in the West, as in anywhere else in the world, small social cliques evolved, mostly based upon the life style of British country gentry, and the usual St. James-type clubs were established by professional men in the city. The diaries of the wives of the pioneers are full of references to the gay social life centred upon Government House. The dinners, the dances, the visiting cards, and all the exaggerated etiquettes of the period. But, when the ball was over, the most dazzling of debutantes would go home cheerfully to round up the cows, to turn a mangle or a milk churn.

When the time came for the city of Perth to be

proclaimed, the instinctive ceremonial gesture chosen was the chopping down of a tree on a spot in what is now Barrack Street close by the Town Hall. They handed the axe to Mrs. Dance, wife of an army officer of the garrison, who swung it with easy familiarity.

A story that illustrates the background from which today's West Australian has grown is about the English businessman who strode down the first-class gangway of a P & O liner at Fremantle. He was of pretty much the same class and type of Briton who had so quickly learned to throw away the fly whisk and pick up a shovel only a few brief years before. A man thoughtlessly accustomed by his Old World environment to the attention of porters, to the respectful touch of the cap, and to the iniquitous tip.

When he spotted his luggage haphazardly piled up on the wharf he demanded of the first wharf worker he saw, and in the tones of an officer speaking to a private:

> "Look here, who's going to deal with all this luggage?"
> Said the wharf worker, slowly rolling a cigarette with the care of a craftsman engaged upon a delicate masterpiece:
> "Ooze izzit?"
> "It's mine"
> "An yer want to know ooze gunna shift it eh?"
> "Yes"
> "You are, mate, that's who."

Whether the modern West Australian is driving a massive earth-mover on a Pilbara iron ore mine, fishing for rock lobster off the Abrolhos Islands, or herding sheep on the Esperance Plain—places farther apart than London and Rome—his character remains the same. Even his antecedents seem to have little effect against the overwhelming influence of the West Australian way of life. In a magazine article I wrote on this subject I said:

> "The extraordinary thing now is that the West Australian citizen in, say, Kununurra, among cotton fields, crocodiles, flying foxes, and paw paws, is exactly the same type of person, in tastes, tones, and outlook as the one you will find more than two thousand kilometres south, in Albany, where they hunt whales, or in Esperance where Antarctica is just over the horizon. In any of these, whether it's Kununurra, Kalgoorlie, Perth, or the Pilbara, the speech, the bearing, the philosophy and the basic decency is just the same. Whether a man's accent hints at Scottish, English, Italian, or Dutch ancestry, makes little difference, for that man, whatever his antecedents, is now, and will be for evermore, a West Australian."

The West Australian community in this last quarter of the 20th century, is increasingly multi-racial. A recent newsletter of The Good Neighbour Council of W.A. mentioned, as well as the more expected Italians, Greeks and Yugoslav groups, a W.A. Ceylon Association, a Dutch Society, a Portuguese Club, a Burmese Association, an Indian Society, and a Mauritian Association. There are communities of Spaniards, Turks, Armenians, and Albanians; there are Texan cattlemen at Esperance on the Bight, and Carolina cotton-growers at Kununurra near the Timor Sea.

At the last count something like one Australian citizen in every eight was born somewhere other than Australia. The Nazi racial tyrannies of the late 1930s started a trickle of emigration and the tragic post-war incidence of displaced persons increased the trickle to a flood in the years immediately after World War II. The great mineral boom in the West in the 1960s brought hordes of eager young men from Southern Europe looking for high-paying jobs in the Pilbara and elsewhere.

Shamefacedly sweeping the old White Australia Policy under the Canberra carpet, Australia has since regularly offered sanctuary to refugees from Korea, Vietnam, Timor, Indonesia, and even Libya.

Nowhere is the impact of the new multi-racialism so dramatically apparent as in Perth. Until World War II the capital, with a population of around 250,000, looked to European visitors like a movie set for a Dodge City quick-draw saga, and a stranger in town, with his pink northern hemisphere complexion and his strangely cut clothes was as obvious as if he had been a brontosaurus.

Once, when I was on a newspaper assignment in New York, I met Jack Dempsey, the great heavyweight boxing champion, in his restaurant on Broadway. Dempsey had visited Perth during World War II while serving with the US Navy and he said to me:

"From Perth eh? I'll never forget Perth, that's the place where they don't bother to lock their hotel rooms."

It was true in those old days. Hotel rooms, cars, even houses were often left unlocked, and though major crime, when it did occur, had a way of being bizarre, in general the crime reporters had a lean time.

The pre-war social habits and customs of this traditionally Anglo-Saxon settlement in Western Australia were strictly conservative and not a little puritanical. The word for the colonial boy in Western Australia was mild, not wild. It seems to me, in retrospect, that the breakthrough in social customs came with the arrival of American troops after the attack on Pearl Harbor. Until then all Australian notions of Americans were based on the movies but now, suddenly, here swarms of young Hollywood-type heroes strolling the streets of Perth, smelling of pomade and after-shave lotion, wearing sharp, well-tailored uniforms, ogling the girls, and above all, with more money to spend than any Australian serviceman dare dream about. Until that moment no Australian boy and girl would ever have been brazen enough to walk hand-in-hand in public, but in a very short time the most intimate displays of affection became commonplace.

Now, in 1977, the city is throbbingly alive with cafes, night clubs, restaurants, taverns, bars, and bistros. One can readily find authentic Chinese, Hungarian, French, Indonesian, Italian, Greek or Indian cooking almost anywhere in Perth or its suburbs.

Non Anglo-Saxon names began to appear, particularly in sport, long before World War II and now curious, barely pronounceable names are as much a part of West Australian nomenclature as Smith, Brown, and Jones. Not long ago the Australian Broadcasting Commission's two commentators at that most Anglo-Saxon of all sports, cricket, were Grljusich and Commetti. The football broadcasts on Saturday afternoons glow with names like Ciccotosto, Sierakowski, Magro, Metropolis, Bauskis, Viska, and Cattelini.

As population growth, easily outstripping the national figure each year, brought W.A. within at least measurable distance of the more populous parts of the Commonwealth, sport has suddenly thrust the State into the forefront of Australian consciousness. The Western Australian cricket team, has, as these lines are written, just won the nationwide Sheffield Shield competition for the sixth time in a bare 20 years of grudging admission to the Big League. The team also won the Gillette Cup, but perhaps an even more remarkable feat was W.A's baseball triumph in the Claxton Shield, in 1977 a competition previously dominated by New South Wales, South Australia and Victoria.

In sport, as in every aspect of life in the West, the equable climate is a potent influence, and indeed, it would be surprising if, sooner or later, Western Australia hadn't begun to claim a prominent place in the national sporting scene. The space and the weather encourage the playing of every conceivable kind of outdoor sport and the accessibility of any sport—from archery to yachting—to any keen young person is near phenomenal. Compared with, say, English cricketers doggedly playing in brief fine periods between rain showers and squeezing in some sort of summer season between May and September, West Australians live in a cricketers' paradise.

Play is possible for almost eight months each year, giving the West Australian player twice as much cricket, in warm, sunny conditions, as his English counterpart. This applies to all fine weather pastimes, and golf clubs, tennis clubs, bowling clubs, rowing clubs, surf clubs and yacht clubs proliferate around the metropolitan area. It was W.A's Royal Perth Yacht Club which, in 1974, astonished the vastly bigger clubs in the sailing world by mounting a vigorous challenge at Newport, Rhode Island for the America's Cup.

More than most cities of comparable size, indeed more than most cities of *any* size, Perth—as we have seen from that person-to-car ratio—is a world on wheels. And though it is also one of the few cities where road networks in the main sections are ahead of actual present requirements, this typically independent, do-it-yourself attitude towards transport poses its own problems. For one thing, it discourages the various forms of public transport that are more freely available in European cities, and, while town planners and freeway engineers never cease urging West Australians to leave their cars at home, there isn't the smallest sign that they will ever willingly abandon the automobile. To us the car or the motor cycle is what the horse was to the first settlers, a self-reliant means of transport without which life is unthinkable.

Traditionally W.A. is supposed to nurse a Cinderella complex towards the rest of the nation but, in modern terms anyway, no visitor could be in the State for long before sensing something completely different, a sense of elitism, an almost smug awareness that isolation has its advantages. It is very true, however that there has long existed in the West a widespread and persistent resentment against the kind of centralism, that is the type of total government from Canberra that reached epidemic proportions in the early 1970s, and secession is a recurring issue.

Far more West Australians than would openly admit to it, have a more than sneaking regard for the idea of secession, and they reject it only on the grounds of feasibility. As long ago as the 1930s. irritation at what seemed like Canberra's high-handedness prompted the W.A. government to conduct a referendum to discover the feeling of the people. The result, which staggered observers else-where, was a decisive 2-1 vote in favour of the breakaway, and that the will of the people was not put into effect was due to Westminister's classic manipulation of the Too Hard basket technique.

The matter dragged on as constitutional complications multiplied and public emotion eased. Today the W.A. Secession Movement has prominent headquarters in a modern office block fronting Stirling Highway, the main Perth-Fremantle road link. Secession candidates stand at every election and the campaign can be said to be alive and well. At the moment there would seem to be no possibility of a secession ever being anything more than a defiant thumb-to-nose gesture in the direction of Canberra, but any return to the breathless, galloping centralistic revolution of the early 1970s could very easily revive this sore issue dramatically.

The secession situation in W.A. reminds us of the old proverb that "big fleas have little fleas upon their backs to bite 'em, little fleas have lesser fleas and so ad infinitem," for, within Western Australia itself, there is a tiny, but fervent, group insisting that they have seceded not only from the Commonwealth of Australia, but from Western Australia. On the 21st day of April 1970, the 18,500-acre Hutt River Province, 370 miles north of Perth, led by a disenchanted farmer, produced a Bill of Rights, and proclaimed its independence.

The farmer, Leonard Casley, to whom the government's wheat quota scheme was as irksome as was the tea tax to Boston settlers, then gave the bizarre proceedings a picturesque touch by declaring himself to be Prince Leonard of Hutt. Nobody outside the boundaries of Hutt took the gesture very seriously, and officialdom did its best to ignore the whole affair, but tourists soon began to pour into the so-called principality to buy souvenirs and stamps (as yet unrecognised by the Universal Postal Union).

When migrants to Western Australia arrive, often only after the most agonising decisions to abandon the Old World for the New, the question they are always asked is what most influenced them

71

to take such a drastic step. And the answer always is "To give our children a better chance than we had."

It is a noble, unselfish motive that will certainly, no matter how heartbreaking the assimilation process, be richly rewarded, for nowhere on this bothered and bewildered earth is there any place where the child of today has a better chance of becoming the happy, prosperous citizen of tomorrow than in this golden State of Western Australia.

The annual Perth Cup.

Kings Park international tennis.

Wine stomping at the Swan Valley wine festival.

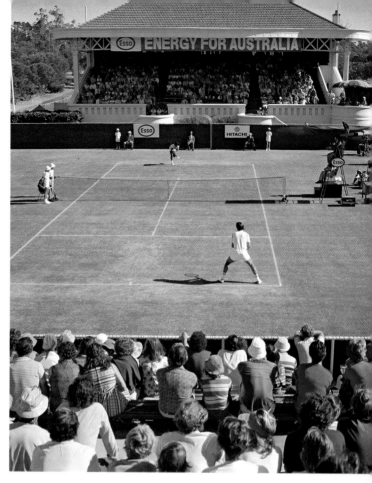

W.A. Ballet Co. at the Playhouse.

Previous page: Festival of Perth, a free concert in the Supreme Court Gardens.

Organ recital in Winthrop Hall, University of W.A.

Above left: Women's memorial, Kings Park.

Above right: Raku pottery by Joan Campbell.

Lower right: Eric Car, silversmith and jeweller.

You've got to be tough to stay on . . .
travelling rodeos still draw the country
crowds.

Anzac Day parade, Perth.

A solid rank of archers at Perry Lakes.
Golfing at South Perth.

A beer can boatracer on the Swan River.

Annual blessing of the fishing fleet, Fremantle.

The land yachts can reach as much as 100 km an hour racing on Lake Lefroy, Kambalda's salt lake.

Right: Apollo & Siska fighting it out at Cockburn Sound.

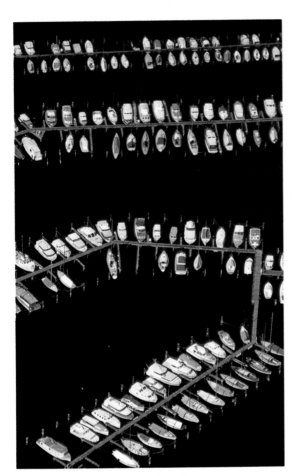

Even the vast waters of the Swan have their traffic problems with all the weekend sailors.

Hang gliding has caught on in Perth.

Left: Prawning trawlers leave at dusk to
fish in Exmouth Gulf.

Above: Everybody is fishing at Exmouth.

Cleaning the catch at Broome.

91

While the sun sets in the west, they wait for the one that got away, or the perfect wave.

On the beach.

Pearl hunting at the Broome festival.

Lower left: Esperance harbour.

Fishing at the mouth of the Murchison, Kalbarri.

Gliding in the Pilbara, hundreds of miles
from anywhere.

Above: An oasis in the desert, Walkabout
Hotel, Port Hedland.

Karratha airport, serving one of the fastest
growing areas in the Pilbara.

Faces of the West.

Above left: Ord River farmer.
Lower left: Exmouth fisherman.

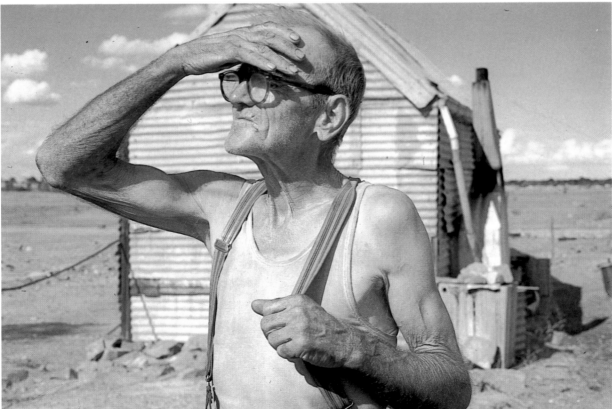

Above right: Retired Police tracker, Kununurra.

Lower right: Ex-goldfields prospector.

More faces of the West.

Riding. Horses played a vital part in
opening up Western Australia, and riding is
still a popular pastime.

Riding teacher at Trickle Creek, Darling
Ranges.

Above right: Trekking through the Darling
Ranges.

Lower left: Kimberley stockman.

Lower right: Andalusian stallion from
El Caballo Blanco.

The University Campus, showing Winthrop
Hall, at Crawley.

Left: The holiday pilgrimage, The Rottnest
Hotel.

George Haynes.

Bob Juniper.

Art takes its place in many forms in
Western Australia.
Body painting by aboriginal dancer.

Chinatown, Broome.

Economy
Mining, industry and the man on the land
Don Lipscombe

As its production base broadens, Western Australia is gradually becoming insulated from the booms and busts that have patterned its economic history. Nowhere in the developed world has a higher ratio of resources to population. And while this resources wealth, combined as it is with political stability, has given West Australians their high living standards and expectations, it focusses on a population that passed the 1 million mark only in 1970. As investment fluctuates between the recent norm of $1 million a day up towards double and triple this level, with new projects being generated, pressures on back-up capacities become intense—the familiar boom symptoms. But two factors are helping the West Australian luck to hold: demand for what the State produces has been picking up relatively slowly, buying time for the still-immature economic system to digest the extra throughput; and meanwhile the economic fabric itself is becoming broader and more resilient. As well, West Australian political and business management is proving itself more than equal to this period of innovation that has become the prerequisite of the next general upturn. As a result, there can be few places with a more promising future.

Cockburn Sound may be the hub of Western Australia's heavy industry, but it still makes a good sheltered place for weekend sailing.

Roughnecks on the drilling platform of the
Regional Endeavour.

Steel man, Kwinana.

Following page: Australian Iron and Steel
complex, Kwinana.

Previous page, far left: BP Refinery, Kwinana.

Oil exploration of the North West Shelf.

Middle: The rig *Regional Endeavour*, drilling
north of Dampier.

Above right: Smoke for the roughneck.

Driller.

Deep sea diver.

Previous page, left: Molten pig iron.
Right: Red hot pellets, waiting to be exported.

Giant karri tree.
Giant jarrah and karri logs at timber yard.
Lower right: The controversial wood chip.
Following page: The karri forest.
Scene near Pemberton, timber country.

The timber cutter.

Trucking timber out of the karri forest near
Pemberton.

St George's Terrace the financial
centre of the State.

If Australia is The Lucky Country, as Donald Horne persuasively argues that it is, then Western Australia is the lucky State within this commonwealth. It is an economic frontier contemporary and civilised—but an outpost all the same. And like all frontiers its economic pattern is one of quantum leaps; which is really a pompous way of saying booms, and they often become boom-and-bust.

Gold increased the population tenfold after its discovery in the 1880s. Wheat production has risen sevenfold since soon after World War II, when agricultural scientists extended the productive acreage. Iron output rose fiftyfold in the first decade of Pilbara exports, making the region the biggest single factor in world iron ore trade. Each leap generated its own economic boom, a spinoff that transformed the community for a time. And these phases are the most distinctive mileposts in the region's economic progress.

After having been overawed by the Australian east coast Establishment, some West Australians are tending to become brash at their achievements. Politicians boast that the West keeps Eastern States' cash registers jangling, that its exports have pulled Australia through more than one recession and will do it again, and that the wealth that comes out of the West Australian dirt is the stuff that keeps the national economic heart pumping.

Often this confidence ebbs. It's a fragile thing, far from fully grown. So when the headlines out of London, New York, Tokyo or the east coast capitals are gloomy, the West Australian bottom lip trembles. It takes an enthusiastic outsider to come in and get the pecker up again; for what other people think of their State is important to West Australians.

Phillip Dunkley, managing director of the London-based engineering group Mitchell Cotts, asserts that "the world economic recovery really starts here". In Perth early in 1977, at a time when the front end of the resources-based upturn was starting to stir, he said: "The pre-investment decisions that give Western Australia its present air of sparkling confidence are being made in anticipation of an up-turn in outlook that will be reflected in 1979," iron as the basic building block of steel, itself the essential ingredient of industrial expansion.

Conditioned for decades to thinking of themselves as inhabitants of the Cinderella State, West Australians are uneasy with optimistic enthusiasts like Ian MacGregor. "For their numbers, West Australians have achieved more than any such group in the world," he said as chairman and chief executive officer of the US mining company Amax, the most pervasive of the many transnational groups working in the State. "Every time I come to Perth I'm impressed all over again." MacGregor at the time was also chairman of the American Mining Congress and its motto might well apply to the West: From the earth, a better life . . .

For the distinctive lifestyle is an ingredient in the West's economic equations although no numbers can be put on the blue skies and the glittering white beaches that are the tangibles of a lotus-land, often seductive enough to hold West Australians at home when more rewarding jobs are offered or to bring them back after such opportunities are taken. And let's not forget the 'hospitality': The nearest thing Perth commercial television has to a hymn is an anthem to the local lager. This life, caricatured as beach, beer and birds, is an overwhelming attraction or a serious flaw, according to viewpoint.

And this better life comes, indeed, from the earth, from the surface and subsurface of a vast region covering the western third of continental Australia, 2.6m square kilometres of it. Its western half, apart from a coastal strip, comprises one of the world's most extensive areas of ancient pre-Cambrian crust, stretching from the Pilbara, on the continent's north-west shoulder, through to near the south coast. Since the early 1960s, significant new mines with the mining towns they spawn have been opening up at the rate of nearly one a year, with no reason to doubt that this record can't be maintained over a longer haul.

Since Pilbara iron exports started in 1966, and a nickel boom was superimposed over this, minerals have overshadowed other economic achievements. So it came as a surprise to everyone but the farmers in the mid-1970s when the value of farm output surged ahead to displace minerals, for a time, as the top money-spinner. Most farmers run wheat-sheep farms; whole milk and beef producers rank next.

What Western Australia may lose on the mineral swings, it picks up on the farm roundabouts. Wool became the biggest money earner during the Korean War's boom prices. When the aggressive postwar expansions of Japan's steel industry faltered and the iron export curve turned down, Russia's grain crop failed and prices doubled—and fortuitously the West came up with a series of bumper crops that cushioned the economy from mineral price falls. When northern hemisphere grain crops picked up and prices fell, this helped meat prices and wool values rebounded, Truly, the lucky State.

It has become a truism to the combination, almost unique, of political stability and resource wealth, its potential virtually untapped. This has made Western Australia particularly attractive to overseas investment which had ploughed about $4 billion, on mid-1970s money values, into the resources industry within the previous decade, and held out the promise of up to $1 billion a year more in a continuing capital flow,

For the earth remains the earth unless capital and technology are applied to it to transform dirt into resources, the earth into the good life. Because West Australians don't yet have the capital or, to a lesser extent, the technology, these have had to be imported. So the State remains one of the last outposts of British capitalism where foreign money and faces are still welcome. And because the lifestyle is so bland—it might be termed low-key Californian—this comfortable status quo is unlikely to be disturbed seriously in this generation.

Here the theme moves out of the pulpit and into the confessional. For Perth is the world's most isolated capital city, both a symbol and a cause of the State's many anachronisms, For all its economic achievements, Western Australia in a sense has been left behind, accepting without question the kind of deal less developed nations are rejecting contemptuously.

Insularity provides some degree of economic insulation; the downswings aren't so heart-stopping in the West as the world's economy goes over its roller-coasters. The west coast lags in the rat-race. Problems like drugs and violence come later than elsewhere, by then diluted as fashions and crazes introduced from overseas and other States have their excesses ironed out. The moon still comes up white, not yellowed. Few rivers or beaches are tainted, and each summer attracts across the Nullarbor an armada of young men, interstate itinerants who bob around like seals offshore, sometimes coming to land for job-hunting, more often just "surfing for the government". Perth is a relaxed and informal place; my sons borrow my dry suits, I borrow their wet-suits, a typical swap.

And although many regard the West's sleepy-hollowness as refreshing—the good old days from elsewhere recaptured in the present, a positive advantage in a world shaken by Future Shock—the fact is that the West is an economic leader but a laggard in trendiness. For people who mourn the passing of other eras, times more like the roaring 1960s than the austere and depressing 1970s, this is the place to marinate in nostalgia, to find a haven from a world that moves too fast without going primitive and dropping out.

Whether this tendency towards being reactionary is, in a global sense, an aberration or taste of things to come will define Western Australia's place in the 21st century. At a time when the environmental ecosystem is a familiar concept, there is only a slow reawakening to the political and economical ecosystems, despite the long history of resources diplomacy that has been sharply punctuated by recent events.

In this world framework, the West has a role fraught with implications. Few places have such a high ratio of resources to population. Australia itself is an oasis of wealth; the western State with less than one-tenth the population accounts for just under one-fifth of Australia's net export earnings. Ranking high among the world's most richly endowed regions, it is forced into the paradox of being both a developed nation because of this wealth and a natural member of the less developed nations' group because of its role as a supplier to its industrialised customers.

So far, Western Australia has chosen to sit with the rich countries at their club. Yet this attitude (hardly a decision since it has been adopted as a matter of course, without discussion) must come under increasing pressure if only because of the west coast's geographical location on the soft underbelly of Asia alongside the Indian Ocean, widely regarded as the next crucible of geopolitical change. Indeed, a diplomat intimately associated with the State believes Western Australia's high resources-population ratio could, given the catalyst of unfavourable circumstances, become rationalised into a reason for bigger powers going to war.

From the time of early colonisation, Western Australia has traded off its resources for the capital needed to develop them. British money started the resource developments with investments and speculations. American money followed; Japan by the 1960s had well and truly supplanted Britain as the biggest customer nation, and by the late 1970s Japanese policy was framed increasingly around the Tokyo version of interdependence—exporting aggressively, building up currency reserves, and investing this capital to secure stable (and some would say captive) supplies of raw materials. Now American and Japanese capital predominates in Western Australia with early indications that Middle East petrodollars and funds seeking a long-term haven from European and African problems will become significant.

The scenario is familiar. In many ways the parallel can be drawn between North American pioneering and what is taking place 60 and more years later halfway around the world. And although two of the principal motivating forces—American energy and patriotism—are lacking, it's reasonable to forecast that the American experience of shifting the centre of gravity westward will be repeated in Australia.

Here a more recent and equally important precedent has been set: For 200 years the resource producing nations have supplied feedstock for the industrial revolution that made industrialised nations rich.

In an initiative as decisive historically as the Battle of Waterloo, oil producers in 1972 demanded a more equitable share of the global wealth and stimulated the movement towards a new world economic order.

Whether this momentum strengthens or not, it has turned a fundamentally important tide Western Australia's way. Instead of resources flowing towards the financial hubs of the world, as has been the pattern throughout the era of industrialisation, the flow is starting to reverse; money is gravitating towards the resources. And where money goes, so does power.

The secession movement is the most extreme manifestation of West Australian's deference to this trend. In purely economic terms, the West would certainly be better off as a separate State, as distinct from a State within the federation. An irrefutable case can be made out to show that the relatively more efficient rural and extractive industries are subsidising the factories that concentrate along the highly populated east coast strip. For example Singapore is closer to Perth than is Sydney, and with tariffs lowered or eliminated would become a most acceptable substitute for interstate suppliers in a trade that runs six-to-one in the eastern States' favour.

But the reality of the situation is more likely to dictate that the shift is gradual. As the proportion of their income derived from the West increases, the companies of Collins and Pitt Streets—Australia's adolescent multinationals—will find it more efficient to base their operations in Perth which, in turn, is generating its own corporate heavyweights. Political muscle will grow around these financial sinews, the West's power increasing in line with capital formation, thus ahead even of population growth which is already the nation's strongest.

with half the population of Kansas, was producing just under half the wheat of America's main wheat-growing state.

As impressive as this may be to statisticians and farmers, it becomes most apparent to the layman when he flies low over some of this ground, perhaps over the broad plains of Esperance or the light lands north of Geraldton. The chequerboard may have many hues—the blues of lupins that are used to enrich the soil, the gold of ripened grain or the green of new grain.

But the fundamental change is measured by the difference in colour between the dirt as it was, putty toned and lifeless, and the paddocks that have been given the warm brown tints of new life. It carries a hint of the miraculous, giving meaning to those with faith in the power of technology to make the earth fruitful enough to sustain us all without hunger and adding a tangible dimension to phrases like 'the green revolution'.

No statistics do justice to this period of growth. Certainly it helped lift population and boosted exports quite dramatically. The 1945 area under wheat, 613,000 hectares producing 433,000 tonnes at 0.70 tonnes per hectare, was lifted by 1975 to 3.2 million hectares producing 4.1 million tonnes at an average yield of 1.30 tonnes per hectare. In the same period sheep numbers increased roughly threefold and cattle slightly less.

But as is the farmer's nature, nearly all the wealth so produced has been ploughed back. Most have the great luxury of productive capacities paid for in yesterday's dollars and this has become a bulwark against recession and, to some extent, against increasing costs, since in bad times it is easier for the farmers to live off the fat of earlier seasons.

Good seasons quickly spill into the wider community. The financial decision-makers along St. George's Terrace are as concerned for the weather as they are for Wall Street. During the post-Watergate slump of high wheat prices and bumper crops, farmers' money primed a surge of cottage building that affected most West Australians, if only

by enhancing the value of their homes more than those of their counterparts in other States.

Farming, gold-mining and fishing carried the State slowly but surely into the 1950s. In those early postwar years, the west coast crayfishing industry flourished; subsequently these rock lobsters have come to represent the most significant item in national fisheries with production reaching a peak of $22.2 million in the 1972 fiscal year, most exported as crayfish tails to North America.

Prawning has also become important with trawlers working mainly the western king and brown tiger varieties. And in a pattern that has superimposed over so many corners of the West Australian economy, an abundance of higher priced, low volume exotic fish retarded a logical evolution, stopping the proper development of other species. Far off-shore Japanese, Taiwanese and Russian long-liners and trawlers have exploited rich fisheries that a handful of West Australians with vision and capital are using to transform the State's fishing industry from its status as the economy's overlooked poor relation to something more substantial.

But all that was far ahead during the early postwar years when the cry was for onshore industry to move the West up a rung or two from its primary base. The catalyst was the BP refinery at Kwinana, a true breakthrough. New industries have been generated along the flowsheets that emerge from the refinery which has become the hub for an industrial complex of blast furnace, steel rolling mill, alumina and nickel refineries, fertiliser plant, numerous ancillary and service industries, and a big grain-handling terminal for the expanding hinterland.

Then came the 1960s, momentous and heady, a series of superimposed booms that have changed the West Australian character inexorably. As the industrialised nations expanded their demands for raw materials in what has proved to be their last binge on cheap energy, the State moved quickly into the world league for bauxite, iron, and nickel, meanwhile turning up the west coast's first commercial oilfield on Barrow Island as well as the North West Shelf natural gas reserves.

Bauxite in the Darling Ranges first became feedstock for alumina at Kwinana in 1963. Since then, the alumina refineries at Kwinana, Pinjarra and next Wagerup have made south-west Australia a major factor in the world's aluminium equation, a trend accelerated by other producers' cartel tactics.

Nickel's discovery at Kambalda during the 1965 Christmas vacation coincided with high prices and rising demand. So Western Mining moved into a 15-month development programme, at the same time triggering a nickel pegging rush up and down what were then generally known as the Eastern Goldfields, now better known as the nickel belt.

In spring of 1969, a discovery by junior explorer Poseidon set Australian stock markets on their wildest boom since the gold rush. Poseidon shares rose from 80 cents to $286 within five months. New companies were being floated at the rate of two and three a week. A pitch of speculative madness that was familiar to their fathers and grandfathers gripped West Australians; visitors were amazed that office girls and junior clerks were gambling the equivalent of several years' wages, usually on credit.

With only three months' performance behind it, Poseidon was voted 1970 stock of the year in London's Financial Times and became the epitome of the new style of 'famous fun' for international speculators. By the time Poseidon went into receivership seven years later, only a handful of its contemporaries had survived. Some of their promoters had been gaoled and court cases dragged on for others. Most participants were poorer, if not wiser.

Meanwhile the iron industry took off with much the same pace but from a far sounder base. Government geologist Harry Woodward in the 1880s had pronounced the Pilbara region iron country with enough to supply the world if only it were nearer civilization. Lang Hancock, pastoralist turned prospector, had rediscovered the Pilbara's iron ore wealth in 1952 and by 1959 had convinced a British mining house that the ore could be exploited profitably.

Starting in 1966, four Pilbara groups were mining ore, mainly for sale on long-term contract to Japan which was at the zenith of its rapid growth. At the end of the Pilbara's first decade, it had become the biggest single factor in the world's iron ore trade, ranked second as a free world producer behind only the United States. Little noticed behind all these fireworks, Western Australia was experiencing one of its few setbacks. When Kwinana's industrialisation began, the aim was to build up an export base to supply interstate and overseas markets with Western Australian goods. Partly because of the competition for manpower and materials that the aggravated boom created, this proved ephemeral.

The dream was dusted down when the time came to assess the 'jumbo' steel mill concept in the mid-1970s. But by then the Arab oil embargo had intervened, its quadrupled prices fuelling other inflationary pressures—the State's propensity for sharp cost increases when demand picks up and the big-spending policies of the Whitlam federal government.

So instead of being able to go ahead to produce semi-finished steel in Western Australia to supply the Japanese, American, European and Australian steelmaking participants in the 'jumbo' scheme, the concept was shelved. Allowing for strikes and other aberrations, West Australian hourly costs proved the highest in the world. About the same time engineers, for example, were having work done in India because they found professional costs there to be as low as one-sixth the Perth rate.

Many will argue with the simple proposition that West Australian wealth and affluence derives, to a point approaching exclusiveness, from the dirt, (more politely termed the State's natural resources). People in their air-conditioned Perth offices overlooking the Swan River chafe at this concept, particularly those captains of industry on the manufacturing side.

Australia ranks third behind only Singapore and Hong Kong among the world's most urbanised nations. And Perth is considered a classic example of a city state. Normally, a biggest city is twice as big as the next biggest; Perth is 40 times larger than Kalgoorlie, which is second. Planners expect Perth ultimately to develop nodules of growth in a string of cities that stretch around the coast from Geraldton to Albany.

But the real driving force of the West Australian economy is in the mines and farms of the remote inland and north, and always has been. Perth people oil the wheels but they seldom provide any motive power of their own. While it is understandable that this simple fact is so effectively swept under the rug, a blissful economic ignorance, it has its dangers, used as it has been to justify political initiatives for the benefit of the urban majority without counting the cost, and on a broader perspective avoiding the call for long-term economic planning.

The ultimate alternatives are to remain a quarry and farm for other nations, or to use the leverage of the resources to establish more processing and manufacturing plants. Long committed to the second alternative, politicians have been frustrated, paradoxically, by their luck; more things keep popping up to save them the trouble of deciding how to engineer the transition from a predominantly primary to a secondary and tertiary industrial and post-industrial economy. In any case, Australia's build-up of inflation in the 1970s made such considerations academic.

For two reasons, there are good prospects that West Australians will find a way to make this change. First, isolation has made them an unusually innovative and resourceful people; it's no coincidence that the State has produced more than its share of people equipped to nudge national destinies. Second, apart from adding historical imperatives to the movement of power towards Western Australia, the oil embargo provided a breathing-space, a time to innovate.

Given the industrial nations' demand and buoyancy of the 1960s, the State would have swallowed several years aggravated inflation and gone ahead to develop the 30 or so projects with $1 billion a year investment potential that banked up after 1973. Costs would have been roughly twice as high as in the previous burst of development, with global implications. Instead, costs have become more important than time and are being counted and pruned as a result.

Not central policy but the marketplace has dictated a higher level of processing. Shipping more raw product than is necessary can no longer be justified economically. In mining, material that was discarded as overburden is being upgraded. Right down the line, more efficient use is being made of the resources, people as well as materials. Gradually, a more productive economy with a broader base is being forged.

This, then, is the lucky State. Its historical pattern has been of booms, based on overseas capital being applied to local resources, followed by busts— each movement ratcheting the economy onto a higher plane. Western Australia's luck in the last quarter of the 20th century is in the change of world tempo that has followed the end of the cheap energy era, a change that defuses the stuff that booms are made of.

For meanwhile, a new version of the old capital-for-resources contract is being formulated: In consideration for right to export energy, in the form of liquefied North West Shelf natural gas, Western Australia has demanded access to onshore gas cheaper than it would be without such de facto subsidy.

This is devised to attract high-technology industry by the mid-1980s. And energy export would be used to cushion the shock of higher energy prices, cradling the State simultaneously through two transitions: From reliance on fossil fuels into the nuclear or solar power era; and from a predominately primary into more sophisticated economy. If this critical decade can be negotiated successfully, no longer will Western Australia need to fall back on its luck.

Deep sea fishing.

Sorting prawns.

The Abrolhos Islands, east of Geraldton, seasonal home for many W.A. fishermen.

left: The container terminal, Fremantle Harbour.

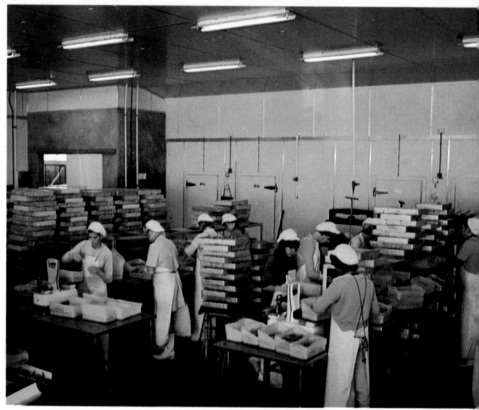

Above left: Prawning trawlers at anchor, Exmouth Gulf.

Above right: Measuring the cray.

Lower left: Abalone fisherman, at Augusta.

Lower right: Processing prawns at M. G. Kailis Export Fisheries.

Albany Whaling Station.

133

Following page, above left: Mustering up North.

Above right: Dry coastal pastures.

Lower left: Country sheep sale, Katanning.

Right-hand page, above: Sheep in the south east, near Esperance.

Lower left: Tailing lambs.

Lower right: Shearing.

Above left: Mustering, Kennedy Ranges.
Above right: Lot feeding, Camballin.
Lower: Esperance plains.

Above left: Angus cattle in the gentler south west.
Above right: The Porongorups.

Farming.
Ploughing the Dongara flats.

Plough.
Wheatfarmer.

Harvesting in the wheatbelt, thousands
of acres east of Perth where most of the
State's cereals are grown.

Donnybrook, home of the apple industry.

143

Above: Grape harvest in the new vineyards near Margaret River, which show great promise.

Sampling the product.

Lower right: Vintner from the Swan Valley.

Far left: Bridgetown, a country town in pleasant hills above the Blackwood River.

Above right: Apiarists working the jarrah

Lower right: Sorting mother of pearl shell at Broome.

Energy.

Left: State Electricity Commission workers with a head for heights, up a pylon near Perth.

Above: Ord diversion dam.

Right-hand page: Mundaring Weir, which supplies water to the goldfields, over 500 kilometres away.

149

Left-hand page: Constructing one of the vast concrete wheat silos at Rockingham.

Giant bulk handling equipment to load the grain under construction at Terminals Wharf, Rockingham.

Above right: W.A. Government Railways goods and passenger service, near Southern Cross.

Lower right: Underground loco, made in Perth.

Above: Surveying, Collie power station.

Right-hand page: Not spacemen, but sand-blasters.

Kwinana, Alcoa aluminium refinery.

Iron Ore mining.
Ore blasting on Mt. Whaleback, the biggest
open cut iron ore mine in the world.

'Wot' about the workers?

Above: Primary and secondary crushers and loadout tunnel.

Gargantuan mining equipment loading ore on Mt. Whaleback.

157

Following page: Ore loading at Newman and Hedland.

Ore train between Goldsworthy and Port Hedland.

163

Above far left: Marshalling yard, Port Hedland.

Above right: Ore loading at Cape Lambert. Pelletizing plant in the background.

Lower left: Pelletizing plant at Dampier.

Left: Iron Ore being loaded at Port Hedland.

Shay Gap.

Lower: Modern housing concept at Shay Gap.

Exploration drilling in lunar landscape at Fitzroy.

Lower: Bulldozer stockpiling solar salt.

165

Nickel exploration drill at Lake Lefroy.

Below left: Nickel treatment plant at Kambalda.

Below right: Nickel miners at Kambalda.

Nature
The land, flora & fauna
Philip Bodeker

The hand of nature in Western Australia is seldom gentle. It is, according to its mood, harshly hot and dry, or extravagantly wet. Its plants, animals and people have had to learn extreme endurance. The seeds of flowers, the spawn of fish, and the unborn foetuses of animals have learnt to arrest their growth and wait dormant in rainless years. The surface of the land has learnt to die and turn to dust, returning joyfully to life when rain has fallen, as if it is all part of an old and familiar story.

Lake Argyle.

Left: Collie open cut coal mine.

Black Rock Waterfall at Kununurra.

An ancient ocean reef, now part of
limestone hills near Fitzroy.

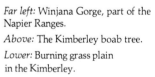

Far left: Winjana Gorge, part of the Napier Ranges.

Above: The Kimberley boab tree.

Lower: Burning grass plain in the Kimberley.

Ord River landscape in the wet.

Above: The Kimberley kurrajong, leafless but in full bloom.

Lower: East Kimberley boabs and rocks form prehistoric landscapes.

175

Tidal flats viewed from the air form fantastic shapes and patterns. They support a rich ecology of life.

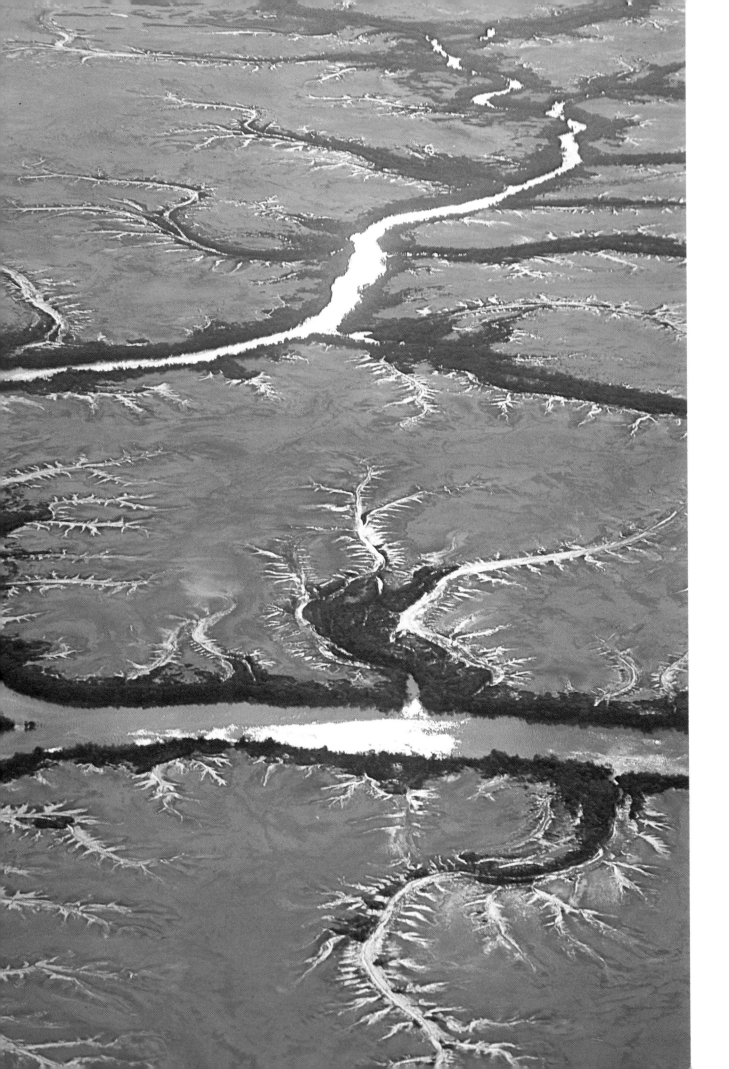

A pelican near Gantheaume Point, Broome: the species is widely spread.

Above right: A flight of white cockatoos.

A sleeping Johnstone freshwater crocodile at the Ord.

Survival against one of the world's harshest environments has patterned living things in Western Australia into an array of contrasting and fascinating forms. Plants, birds, animals, reptiles and fish have evolved within an ancient, much worn land, with soils that are leached and poor, and in climates that are mainly hot and dry.

The flattened land forms are remnants of what have once been mountains, valleys, rivers, ocean beds, glaciers and tropical forests. Today Western Australia is predominantly flat, eroded down by thousands of metres to expose one of the world's earliest known land surfaces, an original earth crust known as the Great Plateau, dating back some 200 million years. During epochs of glaciation, earthquake and land subsidence, and frequent invasions by the oceans, landmarks were moulded that remain to this day. They are steeped in geological history, in the story of the planet's beginnings. They are the skeletons of a land very different to the one that remains. Among them may be counted the towering limestone cliffs of the Great Australian Bight, the monolithic rock of Mount Augustus, rising sheer from flat dry plain and bigger than Ayers Rock, the gnarled iron plateau of the Pilbara's Hamersley Range with its deep scored river gorges and canyons, the heat-hardened folds of the Stirling Ranges in the south, snow-tipped in winter; and in the Kimberley, the cathedral spires of the Oscar and Napier Ranges, formed as coral reefs long before the earth's first reptiles or dinosaurs.

Since Australia broke away from the southern super-continent of Gondwanaland about 65 million years ago and began its slow drift northwards across the Indian Ocean, communities of plants and animals have evolved in isolation, differing remarkably from those in other once-connected countries. Within Australia itself there have been many separations between east and west by alternating invasions of desert and sea across the centre of the continent. Today the West remains isolated from the East by desert, save in the far north where plants and creatures are freer to move across the common monsoonal belt.

Western Australia spreads across 2,500,000 square kilometres, its environment ranging from monsoonal to desert in the north, from cold rain forest to mallee and spinifex in the south. A few coastal oases have become towns and cities in the South-West, one of which is the capital city of Perth. Western Australia from east to west measures 1600 kilometres, and 2400 from north to south. Life forms, depending on their environment, have developed intricate survival patterns to cope with heat, drought, poor soils and devastating natural fires. Because of the State's isolation from the East, many of its mammals and birds do not occur elsewhere. Its 6500 flowering trees and plants are almost entirely Western Australian. Even its own north and south are separated by desert, and with further segmenting by climate and soils, some inhabitants are restricted to very small areas.

Each summer as the inland breeding lakes begin to dry out, a migration of ducks and black swans begins westward across the Great Plateau of south Western Australia. Flying on hot desert easterlies, they cross the sparse mallee woodlands of the Goldfields, the endless yellowed paddocks of the Wheatbelt, and finally drop over the plateau's edge where the jarrah forests of the Darling Range slope down to the Swan Coastal Plain. There, Perth's chain of freshwater lakes provide them with refuge until the following winter.

The lakes run north and south, parallel to the Indian Ocean, between old stabilised sand dunes that are today encrusted with houses, streets and suburban lawns in Perth's coastal corridor suburbs. Groundwater seeping from the plateau and contained in the lime sand soils of the plain keeps the lakes full except in very dry summers. Perth and its coastal plain, with its dry Mediterranean climate, lakes, hills, and broad Swan River estuary, has been an oasis for man and other forms of life since long before the first European settlement 150 years ago. Though within that short century and a half many of the original plant and animal communities have disappeared, Perth as a capital city is still extraordinarily rich in wildlife.

Perth children receive one of their first introductions to nature as toddlers, feeding bread to the ducks, swans and other waterfowl at suburban lakes. Rare and delicate bush plants may be found in Perth's undeveloped housing areas; and in recent years there has been a resurgence in native bush gardens as householders have turned from traditional European plants to the rich array of flowering trees and shrubs that grow naturally in the West. This has brought honeyeaters and other native birds back to the suburbs and with them the tinkling sounds of Perth's daily dawn chorus.

Slow, woolly possums, living in parks and suburban tree clumps, often raise families in household ceilings. Bobtailed skinks and longnecked tortoises wander from patches of bush and swamp to lay eggs in people's gardens. And in the breeding season lakeside motorists are reminded by signs that read "Tortoises crossing".

Wading birds of several species fly down across the Equator, many from as far as Siberia, to spend the southern hemisphere summer picking shrimps and sand fleas round the shallows of the Swan River estuary. City commuters on their way to work have tranquil views of pelicans, cormorants, ducks, swans, gulls, and the occasional fish-hunting osprey. In city parks and sometimes round tall buildings, peregrine falcons ride the rising heat currents and swoop on introduced varieties of pigeons and doves. And along the scrubby, undeveloped suburban beach dunes, small tan and white kestrels hover in wait for lizards and mice.

The Swan estuary teems with aquatic and marine life. From the river mouth at Fremantle, past the yacht clubs and mooring pens of the river suburbs to the broad expanse of Perth Water 18 kilometres upstream, fat grunting river kingfish, a metre or more in length, are caught on anglers' rods and lines; prawns and blue swimmer crabs are netted by amateurs and cooked on beach barbecue fires that flicker late into the night. The city's ocean beaches "run" each year with tailor, herring, salmon and whiting.

A short hour's boat trip from the coast, a chain of limestone islands, once part of the mainland, have become sanctuaries for nesting seabirds, fairy penguins and hair seals. And on Rottnest and Garden Islands, the biggest in the group, live separate colonies of quokkas and tammars, semi-tame rodent-like wallabies, the darlings of thousands of island holidaymakers.

The West is an empty State. More than 90 per cent of its population lives in less than five per cent of its area. They crowd down into what is known as the South-West corner, where the climate is more moderate and the setting greener and more European. In the centre of this population wedge is the sprawling metropolitan region of Perth, an oasis of reticulation and irrigation, largely free from frosts and cooled on hot summer days by the kindly hand of the Fremantle Doctor, a benign afternoon sea breeze. In the other 95 per cent of the State there is roughly one human for every 50 square kilometres, though most congregate in towns. It is this remoteness and isolation from humans that has preserved most of the West as a storehouse of natural wonders.

Western Australia's north and south have separate climates, cold wet winters in the south and monsoonal wet summers in the north. A continuous drought belt meanders north and south each year, accompanied by mild dry weather in the northern winter and fierce dry heat in the southern summer. In the south, summer is a five to seven month drought. And in the North-West and Kimberley, where torrential tropical downpours occur in summer with great irregularity and unpredictability, 300 millimetres of hot rain may fall in a single day, but droughts with no rain at all may last several years.

A dry, enervating climate has taught most marsupials nocturnal habits and so, unlike reptiles and birds, they are not frequently seen by humans. Only the two great Kangaroos, the reds of the north and the greys of the south, can sometimes be seen in large mobs in daylight. In years of drought, some kangaroo species can suspend the growth of their unborn foetuses so that they may be born when rain has fallen and feed and conditions return to normal.

Marsupials of the West, like those of the East, probably developed from a few common marsupial progenitors found right across Australia when the continent broke away from Gondwanaland some 65 million years ago. Then climates and plant life were probably also unvaried and uniformly spread. Lacking competition from the more advanced placental mammals that over took the primitive marsupials in other southern countries, Australia's mammals evolved through epochs of great climatic, geographic and botanical change, assuming hundreds of forms. They ranged from giant kangaroos and wombats twice the size of those today, and marsupial predators like the tasmanian tiger and marsupial lion, down to tiny mice-like creatures.

The arrival of Aborigines with their dingoes across a northern land bridge during the last ice age, some 35,000 years ago, began a new period of change. The weapons of the human hunters and the teeth of their canine pets probably accounted for the decline and eventual extinction of the bigger marsupials including the native predators, and of some smaller mammals. Their firestick hunting methods, combined with great periods of heat that followed the ice age, are believed to have brought wide changes to the vegetation of the time, which although it was acclimatised to frequent fire, had not become totally immune to it.

When European man first settled in the West 150 years ago, the changes brought about by agriculture, cats, dogs, rabbits, foxes, firearms, and the more regular burning of scrub, were rapid and reversible. Clearing of vast areas of woodlands in what is now the Wheatbelt destroyed one of the State's richest fauna areas. Today only pockets of original vegetation remain there in farming areas too infertile or rocky to cultivate, or in State forest and national park.

Food hunting by the early settlers later developed into sport hunting. In the early part of this century wallaby hunts on horseback and on foot were popular weekend pastimes for Perth's gentlefolk. Probably the most tragic blow to the marsupial communities was a sudden and mysterious decline, generally believed to have been caused by a disease, which wiped out almost all the smaller species in the South-West in the 1930s. Once plentiful marsupials like possums, potoroos, tammars, bandicoots, woylies, boodies and quokkas became so scarce that today, despite careful management and scientific work to restore their numbers, all are considered in danger of extinction.

Only the red and grey plains kangaroos, fed and watered by man-made pastures and a network of artesian bores maintained for stock, have thriving populations. Bigger numbers of kangaroos live in Western Australia's vast outback than anywhere else in Australia. And though all native fauna today are protected by law, the two major kangaroo species are still shot in large quantities for their skins and for pet food, under special licence controlled by wildlife authorities.

Emus, found in all areas of the State, have also increased in areas where bores have been established. In years of extreme drought they crowd down along the vermin proof fences where they die of thirst or are shot by misguided pleasure hunters. However the bird which has suffered most heavily by indiscriminate shooting is undoubtedly the Australian bustard, more commonly known as the wild turkey. A big, meaty bird and once staple weekend fare for pioneer pastoralists, the bustard originally ranged the grasslands over the whole western State, from the Kimberley in the north to the fringes of the Nullarbor. By the time white man arrived in the West, bustards had learned by their few thousands of years of contact with Aborigines that a human figure on foot was a signal to take flight. But they somehow failed to detect any danger in the sight of a human on a horse, and so were easy ground targets for horseback hunting parties. Immense numbers were slaughtered where they stood. The killing continued as man moved into motor cars and the bustard still failed to recognise danger in a moving vehicle. Should the occupants step out, turkeys would take flight, but whole flocks would stand curiously by the roadside while shooters lined them up from open windows. Today bustards are protected by a $1000 fine and they appear to have made a good recovery in the northern half of the State.

Another large bird, the mallee fowl, native of the mallee woodlands of the Wheatbelt and Gold-fields, is regarded as one of the wonders of evolution. Parent birds hatch their eggs in enormous compost mounds which they unearth and cover each day to maintain a constant temperature, and which they test regularly with their beak. The young scratch their own way to the surface, unseen or ignored by their busy parents, then go their own way, flying and fending for themselves almost immediately. Mallee fowl numbers decreased as wheat and sheep farms spread across their territory, but today small colonies exist in uncleared bush and neighbouring farmers have become very zealous in ensuring their continued survival.

Australia has some 52 members of the parrot family which are among the most beautifully coloured in the world. Twenty-seven of these are found in the West, though only three are entirely western. As their export is prohibited and overseas collectors are willing to pay more than $1000 a bird for even the commoner varieties, State customs and fauna authorities are involved in a continuing battle against a lucrative trapping and smuggling trade.

Agriculture and irrigation have encouraged population explosions of bigger varieties like the snowy white corellas of the Kimberley, the emerald green twenty-eights and the pink and white galahs of the south. But smaller parrots, the rosellas, red-caps and lorikeets, and the elegant regent parrots, have gradually been deprived of tree nesting sites by land clearing and competition from the bigger parrots, and have diminished alarmingly in numbers.

The commonest parrot of the arid grasslands is the budgerigar, one of the world's best known and loved cage birds. Great green clouds of budgies turn and wheel in massed formation across the plains. At dusk they settle in their thousands at waterholes, many lying flat on the surface of the water with wings spread and heads down, drinking deeply and rapidly, for this is when they are most vulnerable to birds and animals of prey.

Budgerigar populations explode and diminish, according to prevailing seasons of plenty or drought. During the Nullarbor drought of 1975, motorists were distressed by the thousands of dead and dying budgerigars littered along Eyre Highway, the road linking East and West. Bird lovers carried bathtubs of water to leave by the highway for those still strong enough to drink.

In the southern forests and woodlands, mixed colonies of tiny colourful robins, wrens, silvereyes, honeyeaters, flycatchers and thornbills make a co-operative living on the insects, parasites and nectar amongst the profusion of flowering plants and trees. Most famous of the southern small birds is the near-extinct noisy scrub bird, first noted by pioneer ornithologist John Gilbert when he heard its song near Waroona, 120 kilometres south of Perth, in 1842. "Its notes were exceedingly loud and shrill, as to produce a ringing sensation in the ears," he wrote. But numbers dwindled as its native scrub habitat was burnt and cleared for agriculture, and the last one seen alive was a museum specimen taken near Albany on the south coast in 1889. Despite further diligent searches, no more could be found, and the noisy scrub bird was considered extinct.

It was with great excitement that the news was received in 1961 that an Albany schoolteacher, Harley Webster, had found a noisy scrub bird and recorded its song at nearby Two Peoples Bay. Alarmingly, Two Peoples Bay was at that time designated to soon become a new town. Local author-ities staunchly resisted the ensuing avalanche of public opinion before finally allowing the site to be preserved as a nature reserve, where a small colony of noisy scrub birds still survives.

Western Australia is renowned for its wildflowers. Their sheer brilliance and abundance are overwhelming, attracting thousands of tourists each year to the "Wildflower State". As the floral carpet rolls down from the Pilbara to the Bight in the spring months from August to November, stark drab scrub is transformed into soft tapestries of mauve mullamullas and massed vistas of papery everlastings in shades of pink, white and yellow.

In the Darling Ranges near Perth, round pinky cushions of tightly crowded triggerplant flowers spring from hard, pebbly gravel, each flower equipped with a tiny hammer which, when triggered by a nectar-seeking insect, taps its guest sharply on the rump to make sure it takes away some pollen too.

Kangaroo paws, with their softly furred "hands" of finger-like flowers, range through nine varieties from the plateau to the coast. They are amongst the most unusual-looking of western wildflowers and a beautiful red and green kangaroo paw, red in stem and green in flower, has been chosen as Western Australia's official floral emblem. They take well to home gardens and parks; in springtime the natural bush of Perth's Kings Park is ablaze with their dark reds and greens.

Ground orchids, of many shapes and colours, some no bigger than and strangely similar to small insects, push singly through the sands of the plain and gravelly clays of the plateau, hiding so shyly among the more vivid varieties that they often go unnoticed.

The majestic sight of a forest in flower begins each spring, jarrahs first, followed by the redgums, and finally every four years the giant karris of the deep south. The crowded crowns turn creamy white and pink, fifty to a hundred metres overhead, with a dense canopy of starry blossoms that support an industry of beekeepers. Banksias, a family of trees dependent on forest fires for their seeding and regeneration and particularly richly represented in the West, throw up tall brushy candles and cones of red, orange, pink and yellow.

But what is perhaps more wonderful than the brilliance of these plants in full flower is the way they protect themselves and actually thrive when conditions are most adverse. Most of the plants and trees of the West have hard resinous leaves that lose little moisture, do not wilt, and retain their shape even when dead. The outsides of leaves are covered with hard, glossy surfaces, some coated with white waxy powder which reflects heat, or, for the same purpose, fine silvery white hairs.

Members of the wattles, banksias, dryandras, hakeas and others have fruit that are denser and harder than wood, that open to release their seeds only in extreme heat of a bushfire, some not until they are actually baked in an ash bed, and others not until the parent plant is dead. Horticulturists who want to grow these species must first induce the fruit to release their seeds by blasting them with a blowtorch, or cooking them in an oven.

The fruit of the major eucalypts of the southern forests, karri, marri and jarrah, are all triggered to release their seeds after bushfires have reduced the dense understorey brush to a fine carpet of ash, just the right nutrient needed by young eucalypt seedlings. Foresters in the south have used a technique of clearfelling and slash burning for some years to regenerate successfully fine stands of karri; though because this in recent times has been associated with the State's woodchip industry, it has been much criticised by conservation groups and lovers of the forests.

Surprisingly, even the smallest orchids and ground creepers recover, if somewhat slowly, after the harshest summer burn, returning to their normal profusion within a few years. The trunks of most southern trees are covered with a thick, corky bark, most typically seen in the banksias, which acts as a layer of insulation during fires. Some trees, like the marri or redgum and the jarrah, are equipped with a tough underground swelling called a lignotuber, each capable of throwing up one or a number of new saplings should fire destroy the parent trunks.

Relationships between plants, insects and birds are often complex and interdependent for survival.

A native fly of the coastal plain, resembling a bee, lays a single egg in the body of a tiny, cone-shaped native snail that has become scarce in areas influenced by European settlement. Without the snail, the fly cannot reproduce, and without the fly certain flowers like the pink coastal wax may fail to pollinate and die out. Another flower is patterned to look like the female of a certain wasp species. Male wasps of that species are so convinced by the realistic imitation that they attempt to mate with the flower, and in so doing ensure the plant's cross pollination and survival.

Many bell-shaped flowers, or those with long slender tubes or bowls like kangaroo paws and grevilleas, are too narrow and dangerous for the majority of pollinating insects, and are obviously designed to be fertilised by the long, curved beaks and facial feathers of the 20 or more honeyeating birds in the West. Banksias particularly, which hide their nectar at the centre of a bristly cone of flowers, inpenetrable to most insects, are often heavily dependent on birds and in some cases on a particular species. Others are tended by tiny longnose marsupials like honey possums and dibblers.

One family of glistening plants, the sundews, draw most of their nourishment from the bodies of small insects which they trap on minute jewel-like droplets of sticky liquid, arrayed enticingly on each leaf. Along the borders of creeks and swampy places in the far South-West may be found the jug-like insect traps of the pitcher plant. Sitting in small clusters on the ground, they lure insects up their yellow-green to brick-red sides and down into the smooth-walled bowl of digestive liquid within. A type of spider, immune to the liquid, often makes its home inside the pitcher, sharing its meals with its host.

At least two species of plant have existed virtually unchanged since long before Australia became an island. One, the zamia palm, originated in steamy marshes during the age of reptiles and has survived tenaciously during 200 million years of climatic changes, ice ages and aridity, and is today spread across much of Western Australia. Zamias grow so slowly that some specimens with trunks about three metres long, growing north of Perth, are believed to be several thousands of years old.

The other ancient plant is the famous blackboy, so named because its silhouette is sometimes said to resemble the outline of an Aborigine carrying a spear. A relative of the lily family, the blackboy or grass plant grows in dense groves along the coastal sand plains north and south of Perth. Many are more than 500 years old. The sweeping fronds of zamias and blackboys form cool, dry shelters that are favourite daytime sleeping spots for kangaroos and wallabies. While native birds and animals can eat the bright orange fruit of the zamia palm without ill effect, the same fruit is poisonous to humans and their stock. Needless to say, both zamias and blackboys are highly resistant to fire, and fire-blackened trunks are a picturesque characteristic of both varieties.

Thousands of arid kilometres separate the freshwater rivers of eastern and western Australia. Yet once, when deep-flowing rivers spread from the centre across the whole continent, similar species of fish existed in all rivers. Today many of their descendants, though widely separated, are still strikingly similar.

The West today has no permanent major flowing rivers. Though some maintain a trickle throughout dry seasons, most shrink into pools and billabongs. Even the mighty Ord and Fitzroy Rivers of the Kimberley, which overflow their banks by up to 50 kilometres in summer floods, become chains of pools separated by long stretches of dry river bed. Closer to Perth, rivers flowing strongly from the Great Plateau in winter lose force and volume as they seep away into the porous lime sand soils of the coastal plains. Some disappear entirely on the plain and continue flowing towards the Indian Ocean as part of a wide subsurface layer of groundwater.

Fish and aquatic creatures have adapted to these alternating flood-drought conditions. The spangled perch of the north, also known as the poonta or rock trout, spawns prolifically before the last pools of rivers and creeks dry out. The eggs lie dormant in the mud, to hatch rapidly when the next rain falls. Catfish of both north and south can withstand high pollution levels in low, stagnant river pools. The sleepy cod, or giant gudgeon of the Kimberley, attaining two or more kilograms, can switch off its metabolism and lie as if dead under the hard-baked mud of a dry watercourse. Outback people often speak of the fish that appear mysteriously when water holes that have been dry for months are filled by an overnight deluge of rain.

On the Nullarbor there is no surface drainage of any kind. Even after heavy rains, water sinks immediately through the porous limestone layers and makes its way towards the Bight through subterranean caverns and passages. There are fish in these caverns, small pinkish white gudgeons that live in total darkness. Having had no need for sight for some millions of years, they have lost not only eyes, but any trace of an eye socket. These gudgeons of the Nullarbor appear similar if not identical to those found in the limestone caverns beneath Cape Range on North West Cape, some 2000 kilometres away. There, also, are found blind shrimps and eels, and the implication is that similar underground waters have at one time connected across Australia. But in most places today they have dried out, or simply been worn away with age.

Probably the only Australian inhabitants that have not evolved to withstand regular hot and dry conditions are the fish and marine creatures around its shores and on its continental shelf. Most of the commonly seen fish of the west coast are found also on the east coast, though there is a clear division of species between warm northern and cold southern water on both sides of Australia. Two notable Western Australian coastal inhabitants are the western crayfish or rock lobster and the westralian jewfish. Both are much sought as gourmet foods and both are interdependent in their life styles. Western crayfish support Australia's biggest single fishing industry and bring much wealth to the West from overseas markets. The succulent jewfish, which grows to more than 25 kilograms, is only locally renowned; its numbers do not support an export fishery. But it is no coincidence that both inhabit the same coastal reefs. Rock lobsters are propagated by favourable winds and ocean currents that carry their free swimming larvae as far as 500 kilometres to sea, yet deliver them safely at the right stage of their growth to the shallow coastal waters where they mature. Jewfish feed on small fish and crayfish, but are also one of the chief predators of the crayfish's most deadly enemy, the octopus.

Because it has more coastline than any other Australian State, Western Australia also possesses by far the biggest variety of ocean fish. There are believed to be some 2000 different fishes, most of them unclassified, along its continental shelf. Despite this impressive array, the total volume of fish per area of water is said to be much smaller than on the east coast. One explanation for this is that because of the lower rainfall and absence of permanent major rivers, relatively small amounts of land nutrients are washed into the sea.

Yet sufficient nutrients are delivered to the west coast by ocean currents, a cold drift from South Africa and a warm one from the Timor Sea in the north, to feed schools of ocean pelagics like mackerel, tuna and sardines. In the north, warm currents combine with tidal interchange to nourish commercially valuable populations of king, tiger and banana prawns.

The two currents travel towards each other along the west coast, and where they meet is an upsurge of sea life. The most clearly defined meeting place of the two currents is at the Ningaloo Reef, immediately south of North West Cape, where coral creatures have built a limestone platform parallel to the coast for 160 kilometres. It is Australia's longest unbroken stretch of coral reef, in many ways more spectacular and scientifically important than Queensland's Great Barrier Reef. The whole of Ningaloo Reef and its sheltered shore-side lagoon is soon to be designated as the West's first underwater marine national park.

Western Australia has already set aside more than 65,000 square kilometres of national parks and nature reserves, a total of six hectares for every man, woman and child in the State. Environmental authorities are in the process of adding a further 86,000 square kilometres. Parks and reserves have been created to protect wetlands, coastline, sand dunes, ancient ranges and rock outcrops, river gorges, and vast areas of delicately balanced desert. There are reserves to protect whole communities of plants and animals and others to ensure the survival of a single endangered species.

Tourist pressure, a growing threat to once-isolated beauty spots and wildlife habitats, is being carefully watched and controlled. In towns and cities of Western Australia a new awareness is growing, particularly among the children, that nature and human beings must live in harmony, and that the unique plants and animals that have lived in the western third of Australia for millions of years should be allowed to continue to do so.

Deep in a Hamersley gorge, a ghost gum sapling.

The Hamersley Range near Wittenoom.

Lower left: The sturt pea and desert spinifex flourishing after rain.

Lower right: Characteristic rock of the Dampier landscape.

Right-hand page: Deep gorges, sculptured by the enormous power of Hamersley flash floods.

Previous page: View from Chichester Range towards Mt. Herbert.

Green spiky balls of spinifex cloak the bare iron earth of the Chichester Range.

Above left: Whole flocks of white cockatoos mass themselves in single trees.

Above right: The white egret.

Lower left: Wild hibiscus, a relative of the cotton plant.

Lower right: Wild honey.

Early morning mists hang on river flats
east of the Chichester Range.

Dales Gorge, popular tourist attraction near Wittenoom.

195

Mt. Augustus, Australia's biggest monolyth, bigger than Ayers Rock but because it is vegetated, less spectacular.

Following page: Kids at the Murchison. Kalbarri National Park is the home of the spectacular Murchison River Gorge.

Above: Typical coastline near Kalbarri.

Lower: Ironstone pebbles give the vast flatness of the Murchison a wet look, even in desert heat.

Right-hand page: A petrified limestone forest, the Pinnacles, near Jurien Bay. This unique landscape is a national park.

Fire is both friend and foe of native
vegetation. Many seeds need fire to
germinate and afterwards the landscape
blooms with new life.

A white egret, a patient hunter, poised
motionless.

Right-hand page above left: The emu blends
well with dry, scrubby surroundings.

Above right: A pair of ospreys near the
Albany coast.

Right-hand page, lower: A crested pigeon
is part of the northern landscape.

The blackboy is Australia's oldest form of plant life. These beautiful grass trees have adapted themselves to many environments and are well conditioned to fire.

A splash of colour on the sandy plains east
of Southern Cross.

Wave Rock, Hyden.

Left-hand page: Sheoak landscape near
Hyden.

Bushfires, depending on their moods, leave stark destruction or landscapes tinged with autumn colours.

211

The Stirling Ranges, heat-hardened folds of ancient rock, rise from the southern plain. Among their many resident wildflowers are the tall yellow candles of the bull banksia, the fluffy cone flower, and this yellow leafed member of the boronia family.

Following page: In spring, from August to October, the bush bursts into colour. All these flowers grow in the Darling Ranges close to Perth.

Left: Tenacious coastal scrub clings to limestone hills near Cowaramup on the South-West corner.

Right-hand page: Jewel cave at Augusta, formed beneath limestone rock.

Left: Karri forest, Walpole Inlet.

Right: Encroaching dunes fossilised this tree in limestone.

Our turbulent western coast near Margaret River.

Following page: Estuaries attract many visitors. Pelican Point on the Swan River is a world renowned bird sanctuary.

223

Left-hand page: Beach landscape near Albany.

Above: Pink lake, at Esperance, coloured by microscopic algae.

Lower: Coastal sandstone at Cape Le Grand, near Esperance.

Previous page: The tranquility of the Denmark estuary contrasts sharply with the rugged Albany coastline close by.

Left-hand page, above: Lucky Bay, Cape Le Grand. A Christmas tree in bloom.
Left-hand page, lower and above left: Cape Le Grand has many faces. A cold, arid climate has shaped its land features and plants.

Lower: The shifting sands at Eucla.

Following page above: Sunset over the old telegraph station at Eucla, partly buried by sand drifts.

Lower: Cliffs of Eucla, once part of an ancient seabed, rise more than 100 metres from the Great Australian Bight.